THE SHAPE A WING MAKES

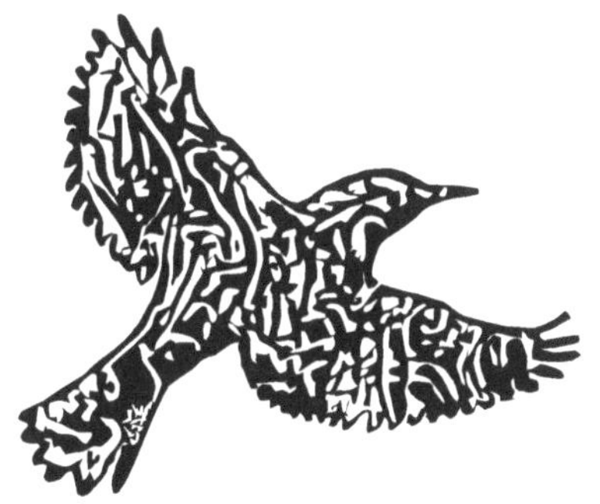

Poems by Fran Claggett-Holland

Art by Freeman Ng

THE SHAPE A WING MAKES

By Fran Claggett-Holland and Freeman Ng

ISBN: 978-0-9906197-7-2

Three Daughters Press
www.ThreeDaughtersPress.com

ACKNOWLEDGEMENTS

"Black Birds and Other Birds", "Brush Strokes", "Heron and Loon", "How Long a Ways to Never Land", "I Do Not Need To Know", and "While Speaking to a Group of English Teachers in a Structured Situation" first appeared in *Black Birds and Other Birds* (Taurean Horn Press, 1977).

"Crow at Ocean's Edge", "Moving Into Language", "Old Man", "Poem Hidden in Bamboo", and "The Untoward Crow" first appeared in *Crow Crossings* (RiskPress, 2012).

"Heaven's Wing", "I, Claude Monet", "Litany", "now that leaves", "Oh, empty ledge", "On Taking the Measure of Your Book", "raven-winged Icarus", "Winter Solstice", and "Winter Solstice in Shadow" first appeared in *Consciousness of Stone* (RiskPress, 2019).

"Aubade for the Quiet House", "Evolution of the Sun Temple", "Flickering Lights", "In Times Like These", "A Sense of Permanence", and "What is it about these mountain sheep?" first appeared in *Under the Wings of the Crow* (RiskPress, 2021).

Reprinted by permission of Fran Claggett and RiskPress.

CONTENTS

INTRODUCTION BY FREEMAN NG

This is a book of poems by Fran Claggett-Holland paired with my own digital art.

Fran was the high school teacher who got me started writing poetry over 45 years ago. She's remained a mentor, mother figure, and friend ever since. She has a part in everything I do, including my art.

As you read these poems, you'll notice that they contain many birds or other winged creatures. They're a common subject for Fran and an illuminating way to think about how she lives her life and what she does for others.

I'm immensely grateful to the many people who had a part in my upbringing, including:

My father, who worked tirelessly to build the nest that sheltered me for so long.

My mother, who fed me from her sacrificial heart.

My sister, for whom the nest was not the secure place it was for me, and who courageously fled it early in her life, but did what she could to prepare me for the world beyond it before she left.

And Fran, whom I met at that point in my life when it was time to learn how to fly.

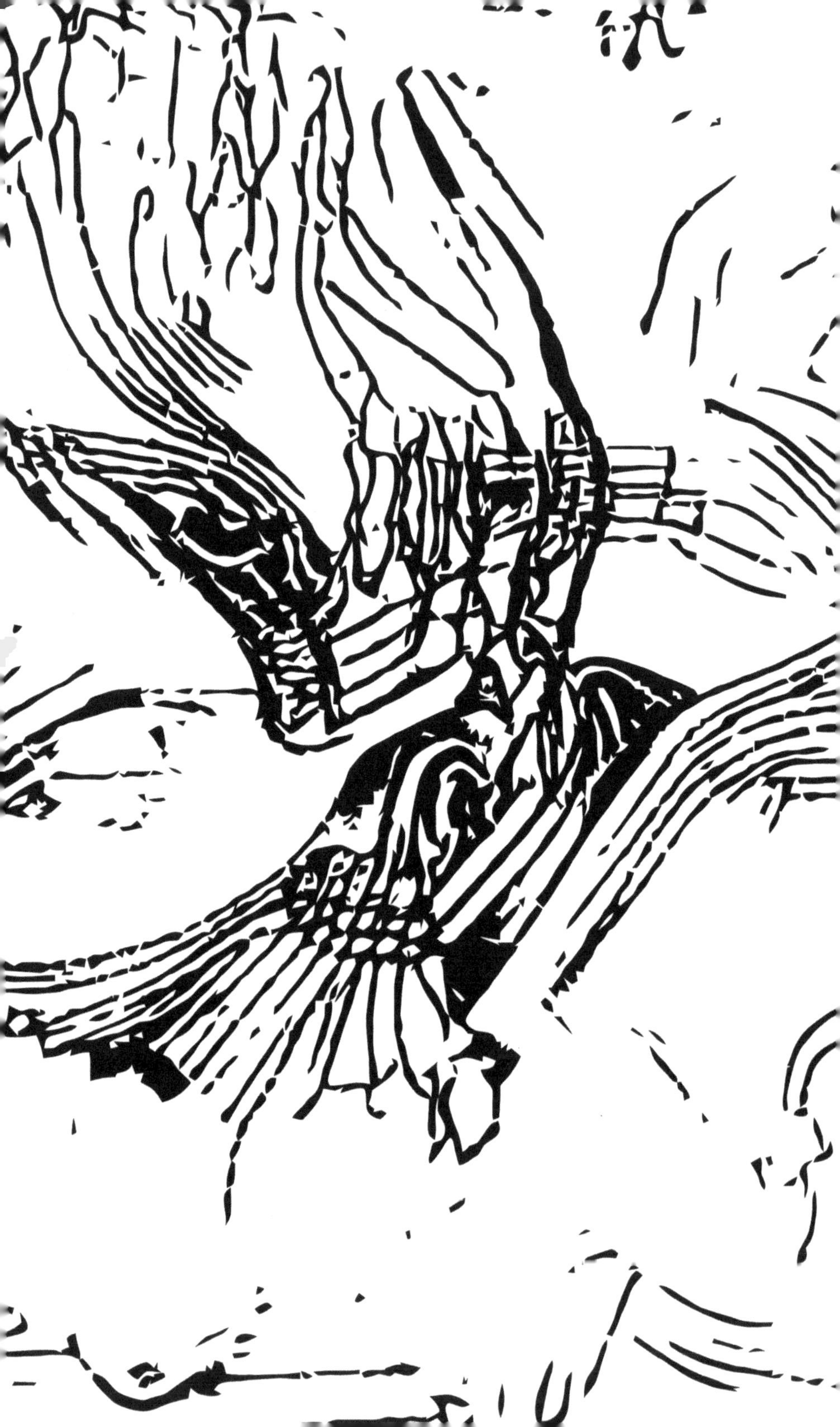

BLACK BIRDS AND OTHER BIRDS

It is not enough to know
the birds
only at noon.

At noon you say
see, it is a tern,
I know it by its red beak,
or
look, the gull has
grey wings,
or still again,
the blackbird has frightened
the purple finch.

At noon, we know a thing
by its color.
It takes the sun —
rising
or falling —
to turn the white gull black.
We must go colorblind
to see
the shape a wing makes.

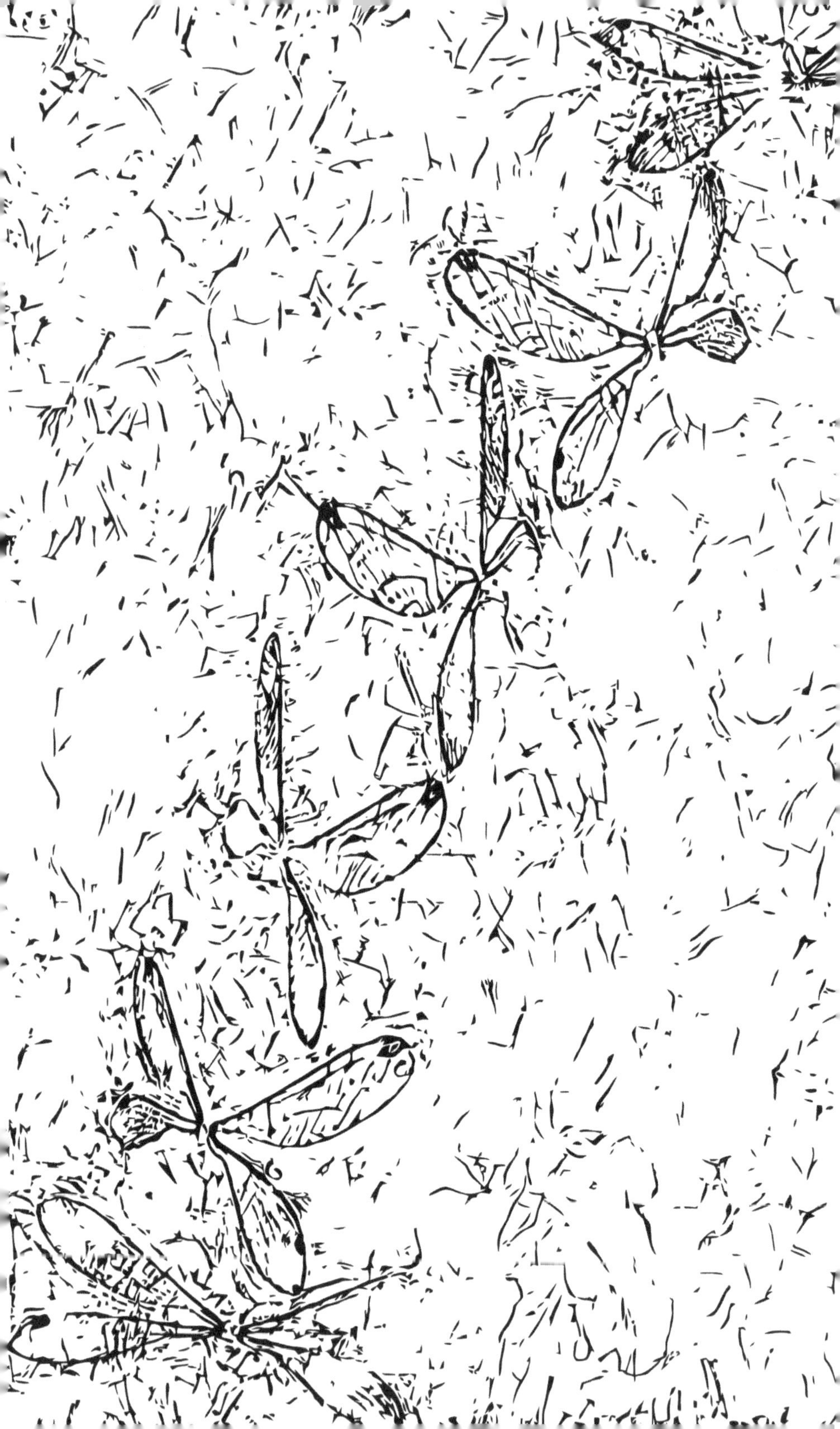

The lacy-winged moth
settled into sand. Sun-dried
wings rose with the breeze
leaving delicate
impressions of her life.

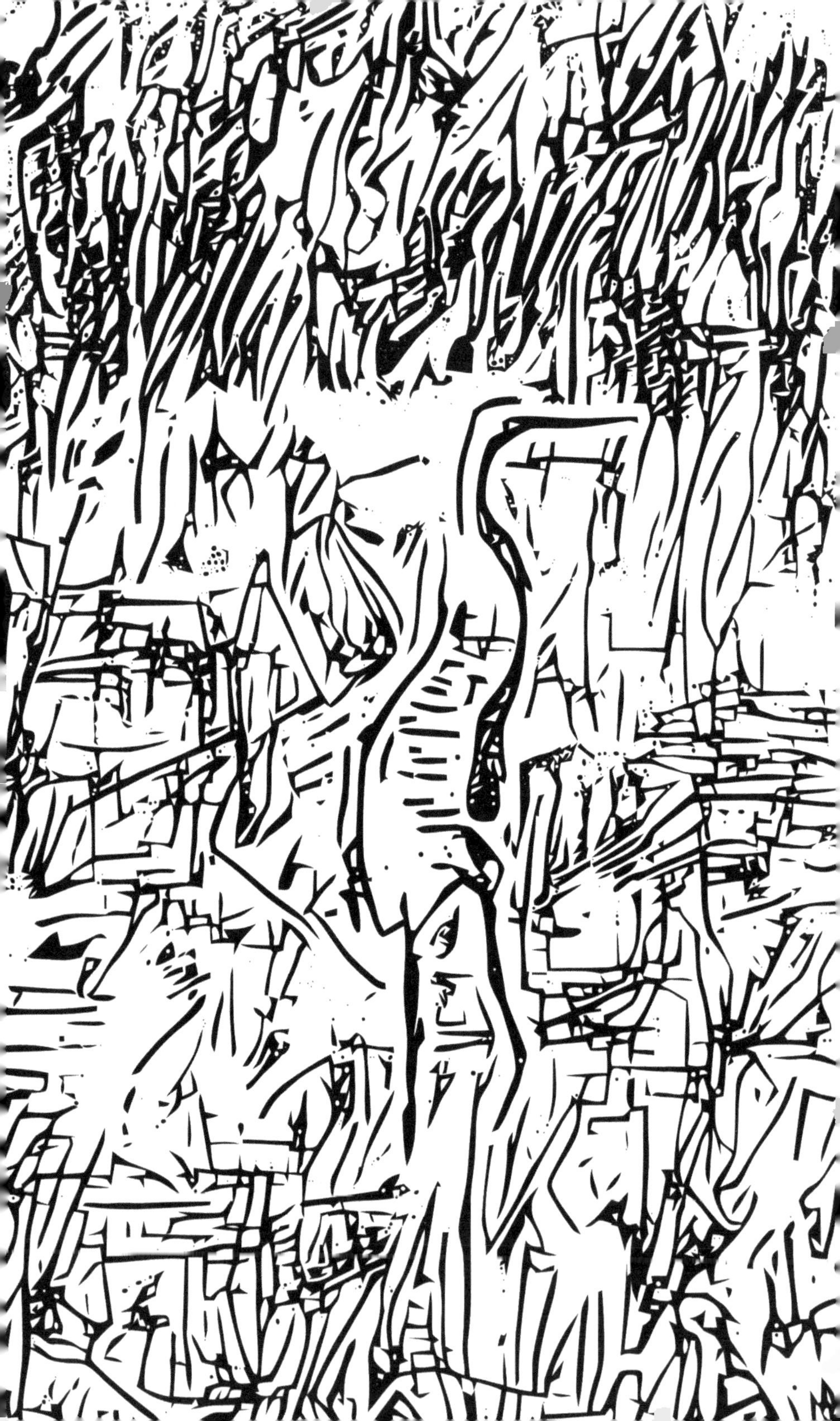

SHADOWED STARS REDEFINED

hesitations we once took
for ordinary
change the tension of the night

like stars at dusk
we and the egret
disappear to the world

emerge in nightgrass
remote as the obdurate heart
pulsing trochees of stress

gradual ambient sunlight
replaces the ambiguities
of our shadowed life

in the uncertainty of morning
we and the stars once again
wait for the silence of the dark

the egret fans its great wings
assumes its poised stature
becomes almost visible

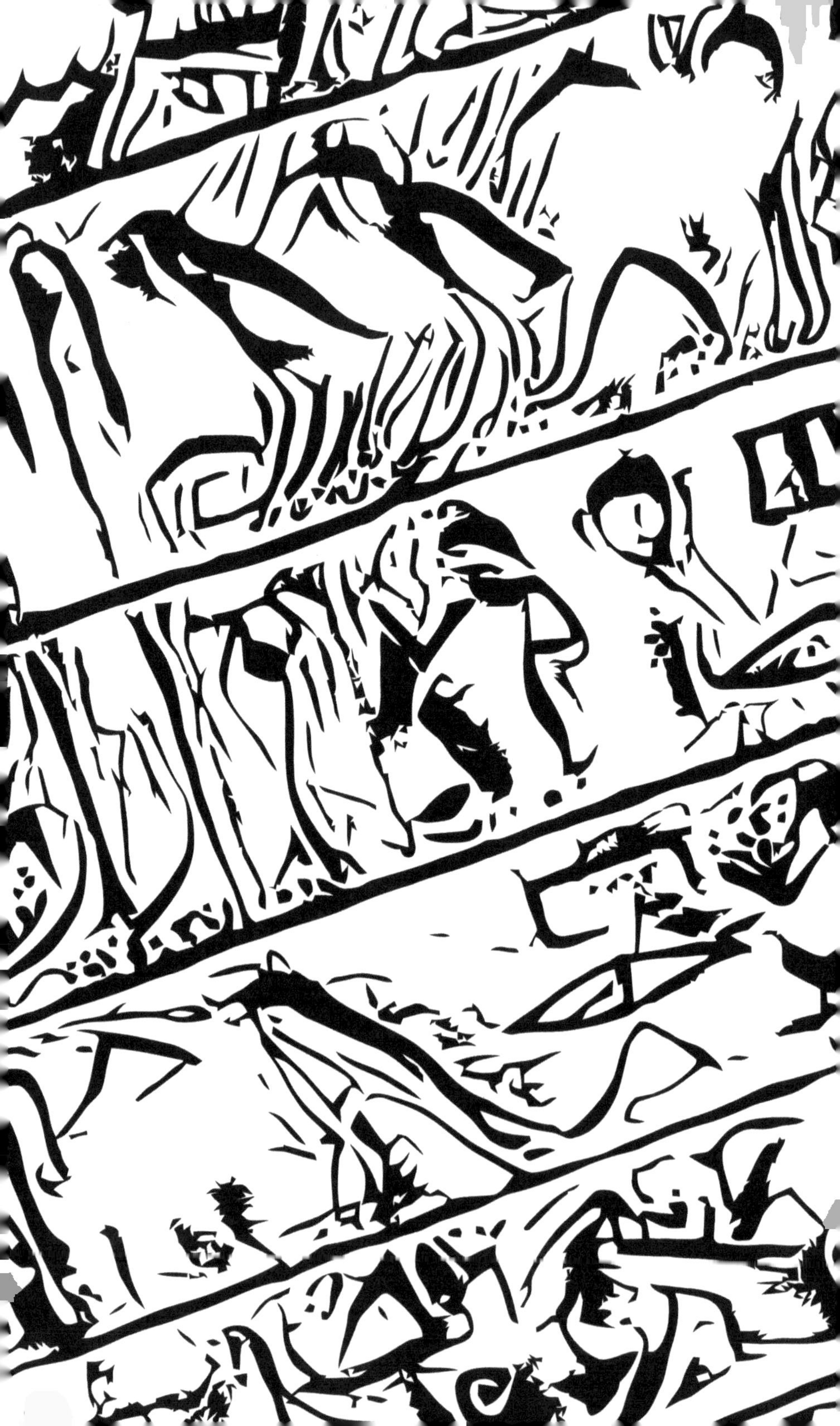

HIDDEN WORDS

I write
I do not know
what I have written
I have written beyond these words
to their shadows
the hieroglyphs that hold
sacred meanings within
I cannot read these dark
marks that still live within
what has emerged
on this thin remnant of
etched stone
there is no translation
for the language
of the heart

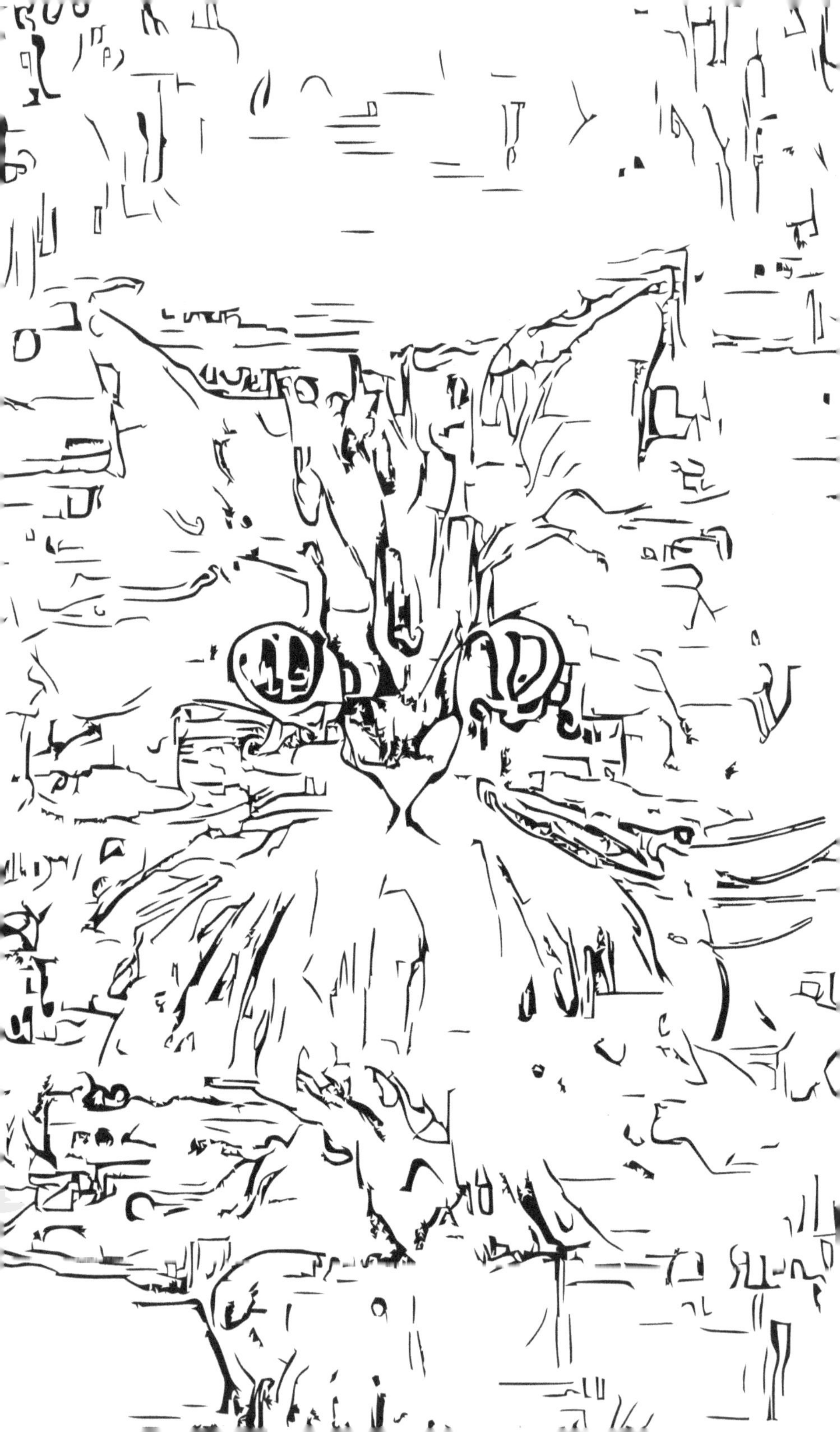

WHILE SPEAKING TO A GROUP OF ENGLISH TEACHERS IN A STRUCTURED SITUATION

(after an anecdote told by James Moffett at Asilomar Seventeen)

mid speech   the Persian
cat   by white design
dropped
from his
still life
formal be-
side the side–
board bowl of fruit
into
my
lap
Demanding not   my touch
but
all the eyes that
had been
before his calculated
leap
mine
Suggesting that   perhaps we all
(as
EnglishTeachers)
might
by design
leap.

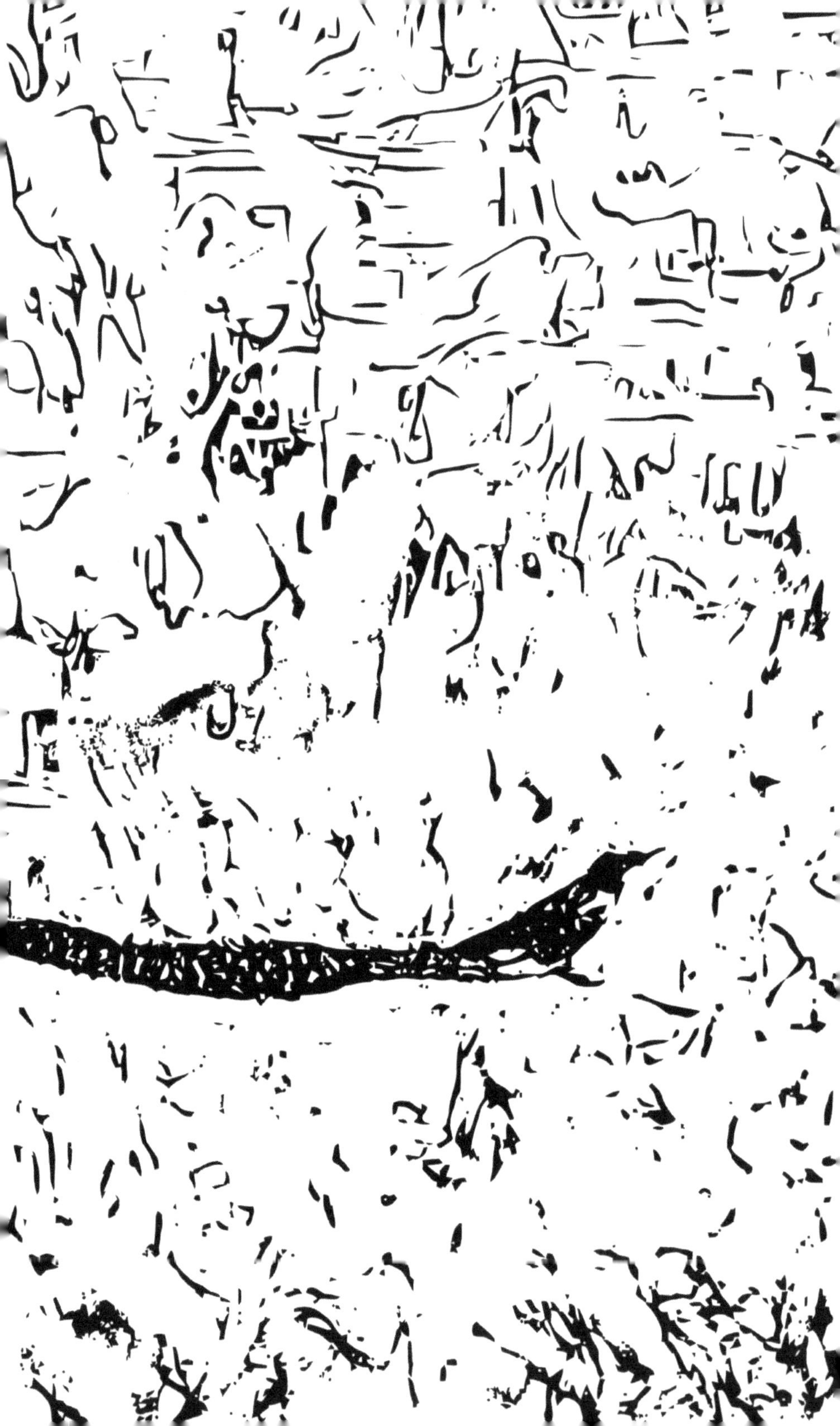

CROW AT OCEAN'S EDGE

I breathe
in the early filtered sun
poised
between night and morning,
water and sand.

A crow
startles my line of vision,
absorbs the shadows.

I watch the crow form
patterns—black, white,
wings changing light,
ink falling on sand.

OLD MAN

Old man, bird weight,
I could hold you
in the palm of my hand,
feed you honey water
with an eye dropper and
put you into a nest
of old newspapers
by the door, hoping,
in the morning,
to find you gone.

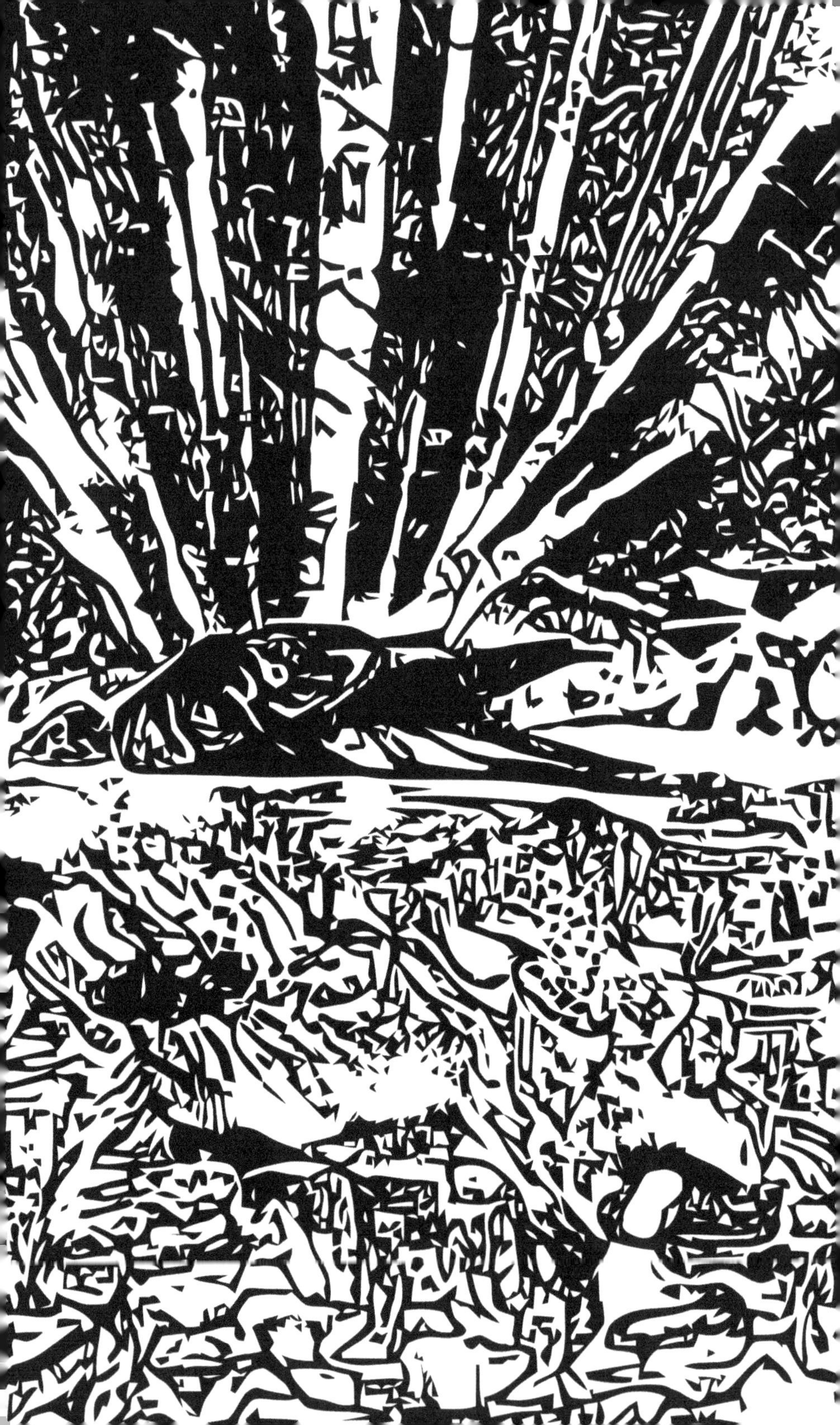

HEAVEN'S WING

a Ghazal

It was the buzzard that got my attention,
Lying there, all intention lost to sky.

Thinking of nothing else, neither buzzard nor I,
Wings of angels thrust broken into the bleak black sky,

All intention lost in obsidian silence--
Angels and buzzard united in star-studded stillness.

Then I, focused on intention, buried my eye,
Seeing deep into the aching loss, while that black bird

Of Heaven, charged with the cleansing of the soul,
Gave up its dark duties of the visceral night,

Lost to sleep, lost to the waking tension
Of the day, lost Oh Buzzard, to Heaven's wing.

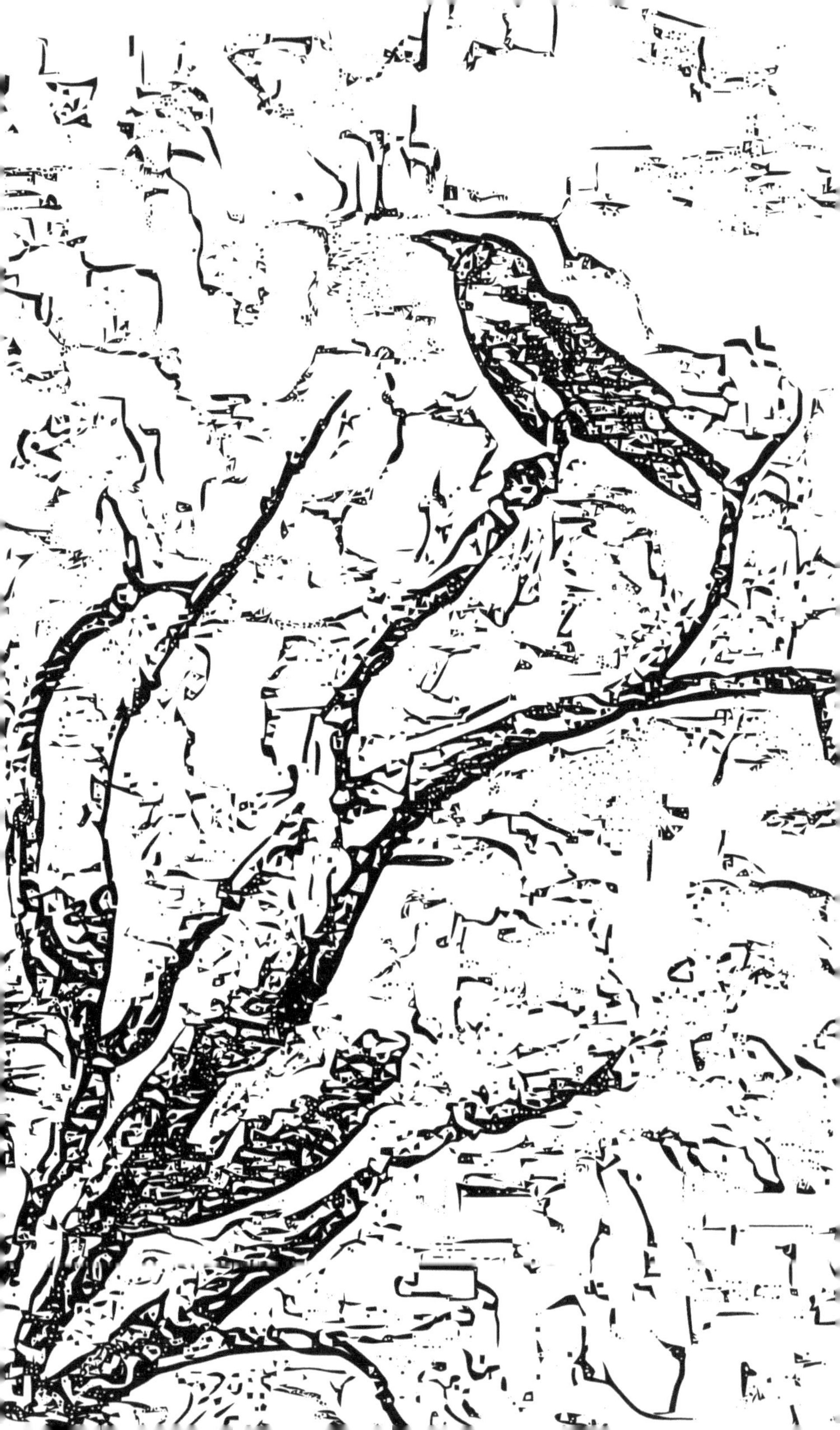

THE UNTOWARD CROW

The untoward crow
sits motionless on the
bleached bones of the dead tree
a still life posed, waiting.

What tremor in the earth or air
would prod that bird to
        shift its weight
        unfold its wings
        announce its demarcation
                from the tree? from me?

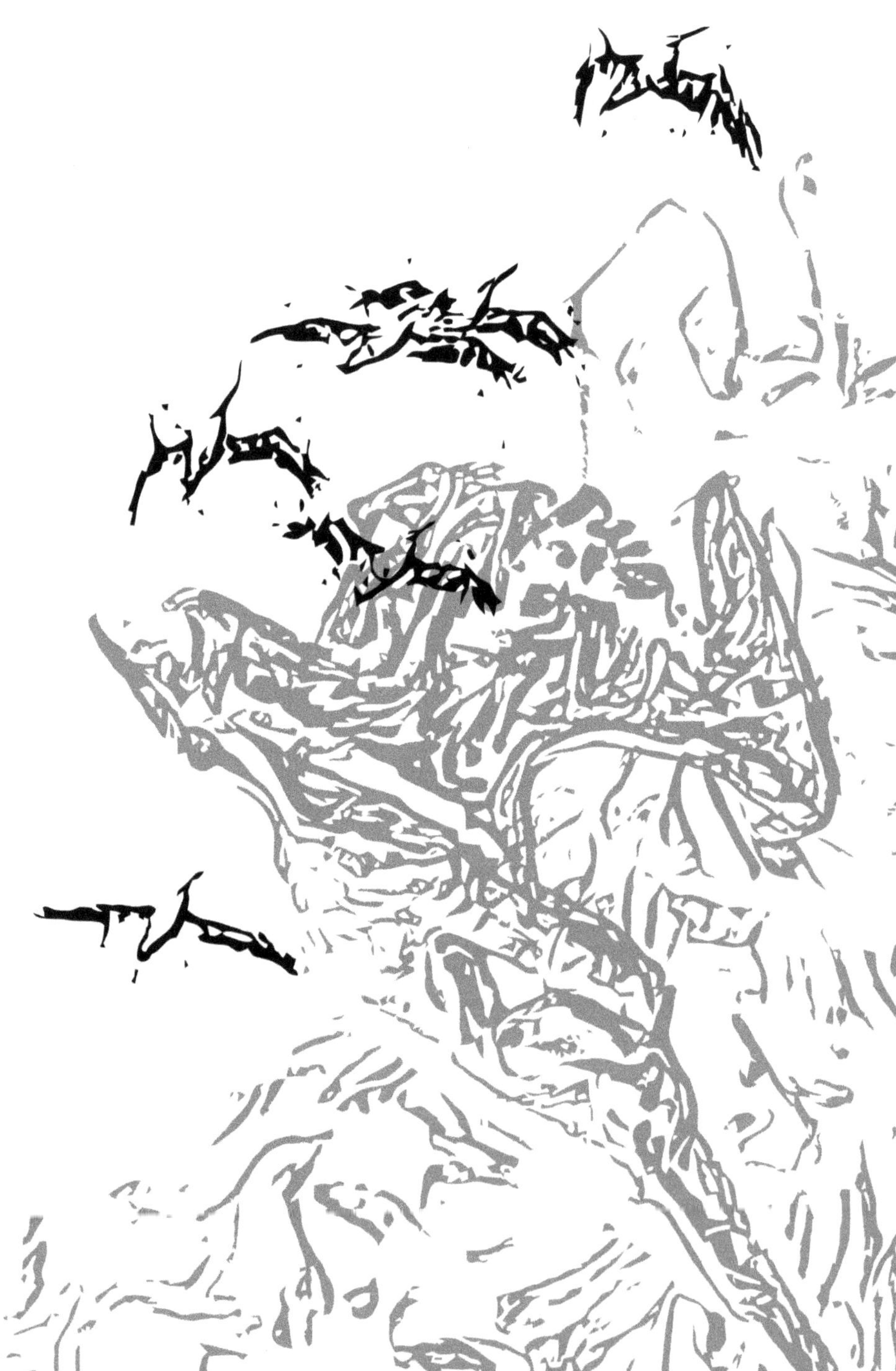

ON TAKING THE MEASURE OF YOUR BOOK

for Michael Franco

there must be a way
to enter your poetry
the way your words turn
into meaning after meaning
into the depths of memory
into the silence of the beach
which of course is never silent
but it seems so when I am there alone
and then the birds come
over the dunes
the tiny sandpipers,
silent in sand
creating the rhythm
of your poem
and far out beyond my eyes
the great white pelicans
and as I watch them I see
how I must enter your poetry
wings folded against the wind
as I slice again and again
into the measure of your ocean
there where silence is translated
into language

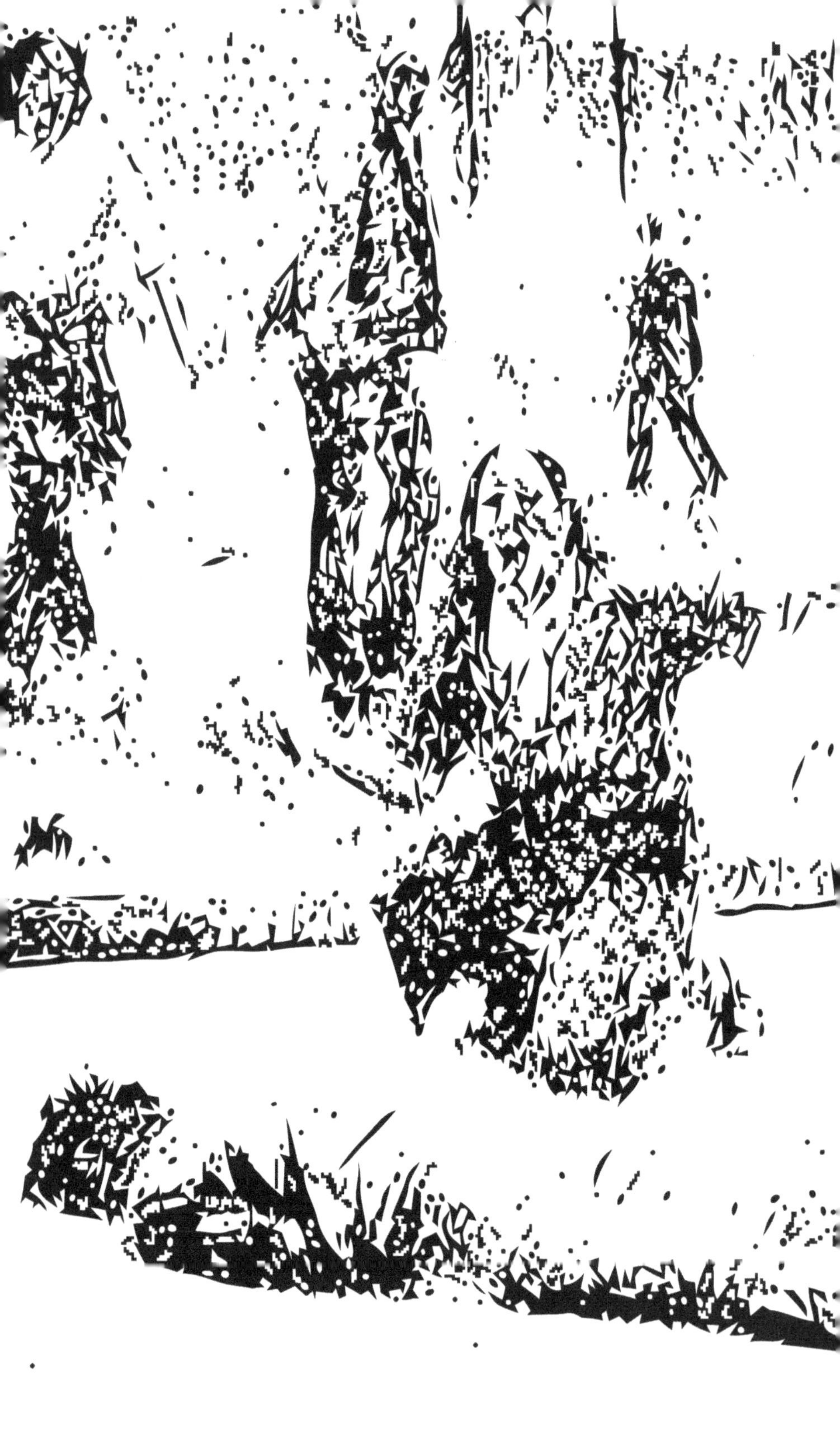

I DO NOT NEED TO KNOW

I do not need to know the other side of death/
dying.
Teachers do not take the hippocratic oath.

We have no snakes
entwined
upon the staff of life.

The oath we take is silent/
sworn
to view
reality one way through
the looking glass.
(Present both sides. Take no stand.
Above all
do not influence your students.

Swear.)

And are there, then two sides to dying/
death?

The living know but one.

The raven screams my oath

stretching his wings
across the bloodied dove.

May 6, 1970
in response to the death of four students at Kent State

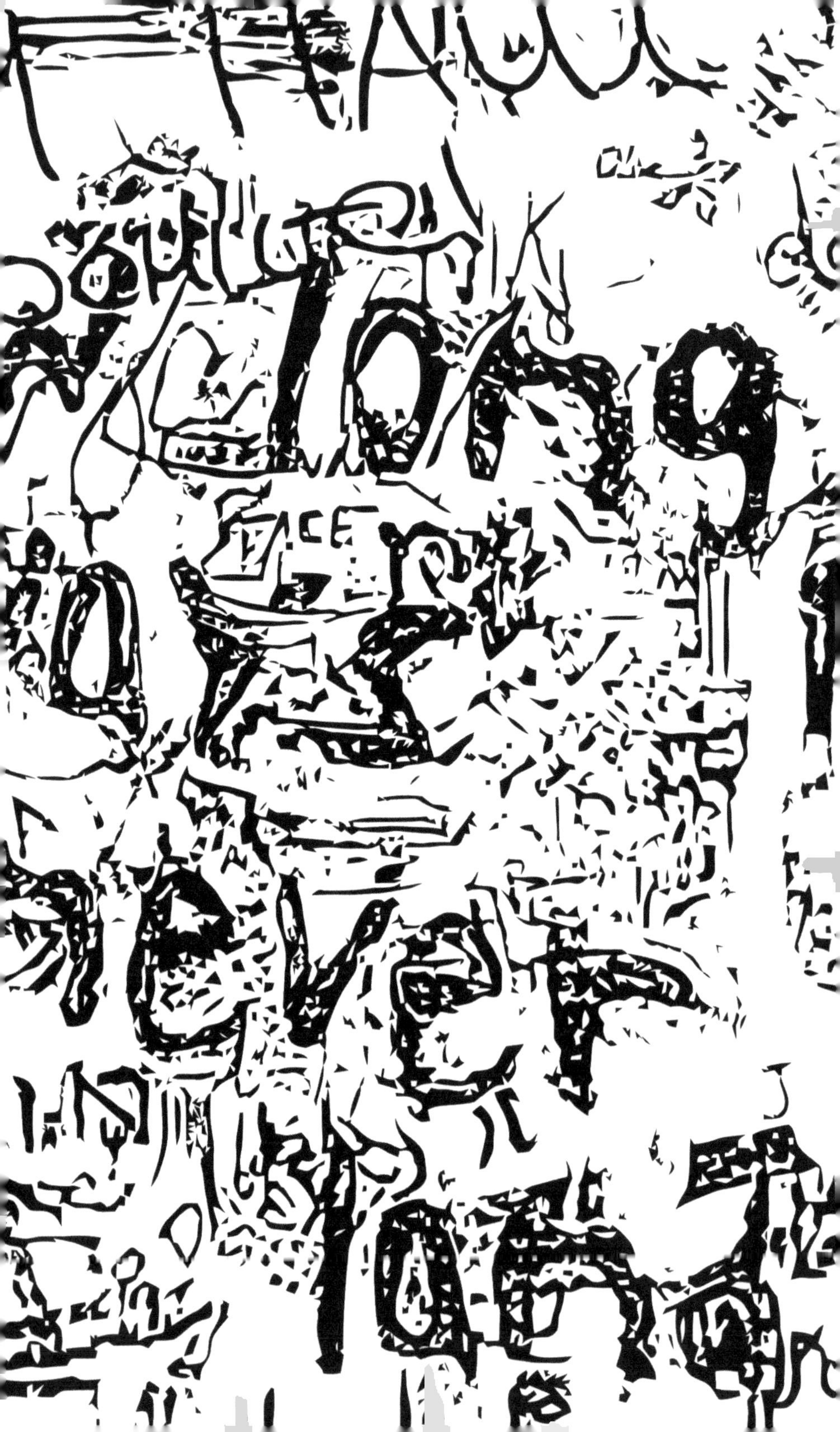

HOW LONG A WAYS TO NEVER LAND

(graffiti found on the wall of a ghetto school)
for Jeanette Sibley

Stone-scratched letters
          high up on the south side wall
               of the south side school
stone-scratched letters
          stretched to words
stone-etched words
               wrung from a voice
          dumb in the white
               face of ruled paper
          numb in the ruled
               face of—
                    in the papered
               face of—
                    in the silent voice of the
          hooded child—
                    in the childhooded voice that
               touches the
space
                    a stone's throw
          between the never
                    never of the broken
                                        land.

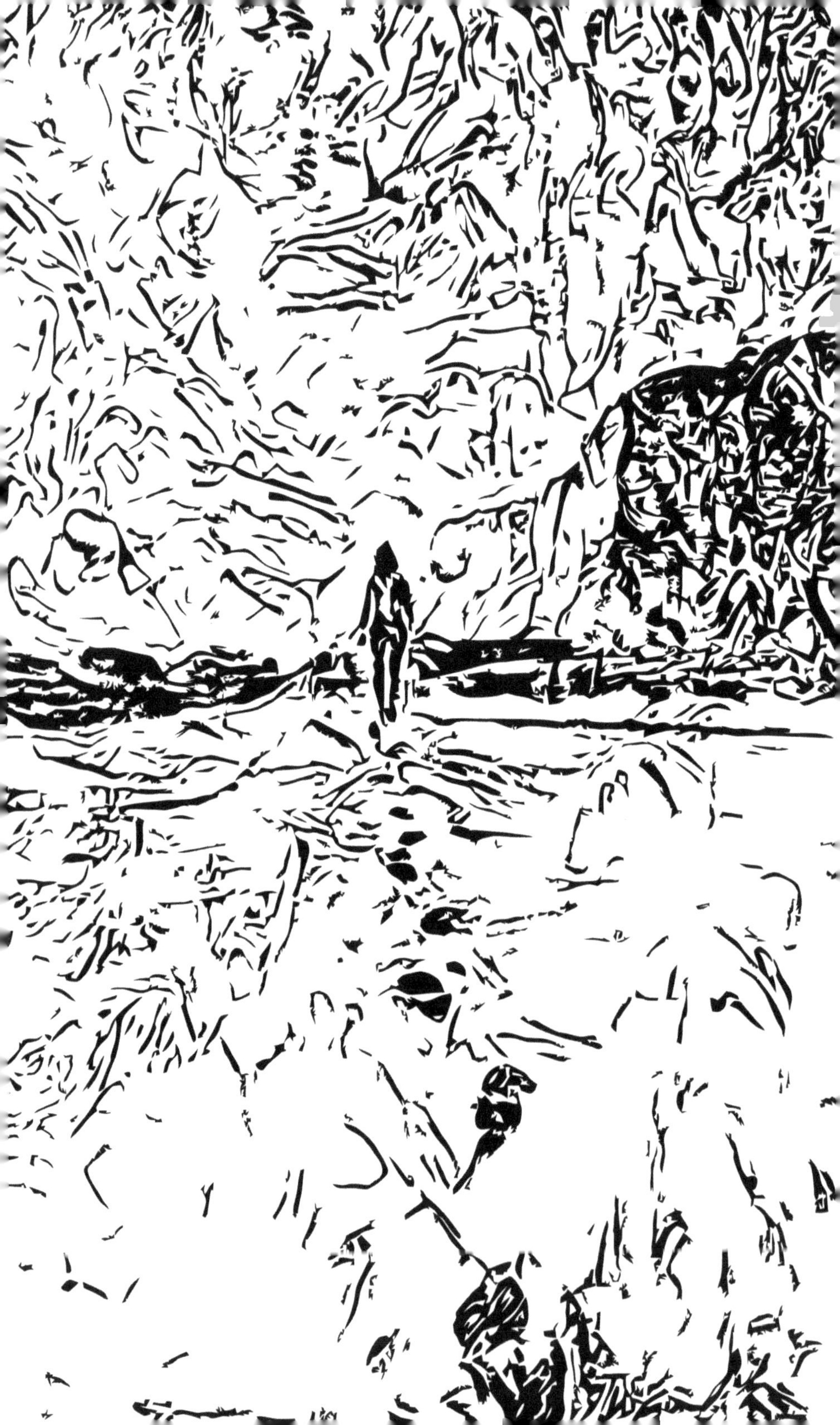

MOVING INTO LANGUAGE

We walk
on the bones of our mother,
shape earth silence
into elegy,
mourn the lost words that
lie with her,
searching
for our own lost song.

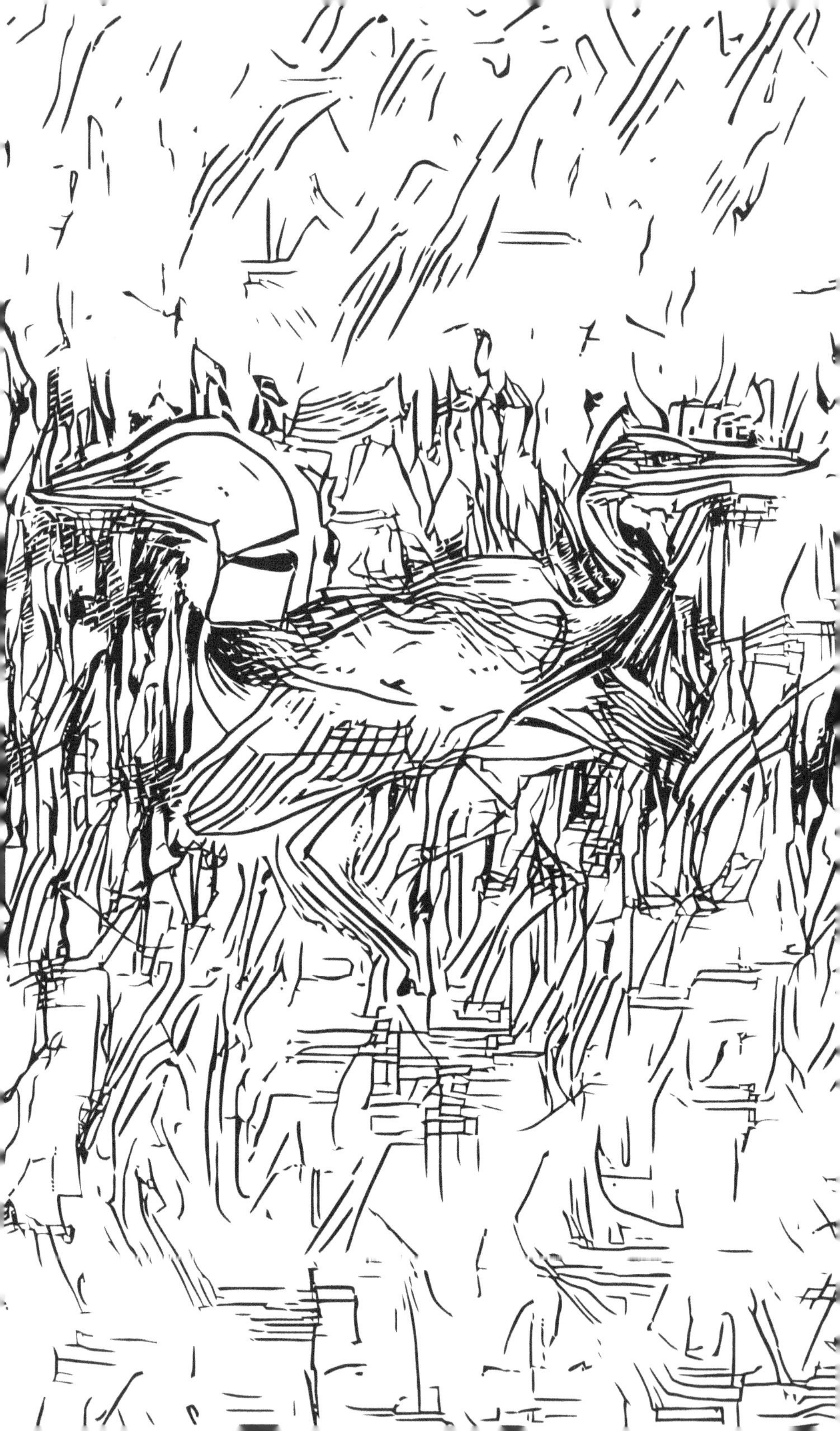

HERON AND LOON

the dream, then:

together we went, Indian style, thru the wet pine,
in search of the loon,
hand held lights diffusing
in the moonless fog.

together we moved,   and alone,   branches
brushing the sequence
of our silence, our
solitudes spaced between
the dim centers of
refracted light.

the loon.   the midnight madness:

who among us could have thought
at noon that we
at night could move
the loon to leave our
common refuge, here
where the river brings us
calm reflections of the sea.

who among us could have thought
that we possessed
the power of the moon, to draw
the tides of madness out,
to free us from the echo
of the sea

afterward,   the reality:

I had a dream once.   There was a great
blue bird, composed
                    on the bough of a pine.
'I could have touched–'

                    but distances are more
                    than dreams.   the loon
                    keeps his kind of distance
                    just beyond hearing
                    in the inner ear.
                    The great blue bird –
                    A heron, now I know –
is silent.
                    I could have touched him.

(fifteen years in the mind, the ear.
                    from maine to salmon creek)

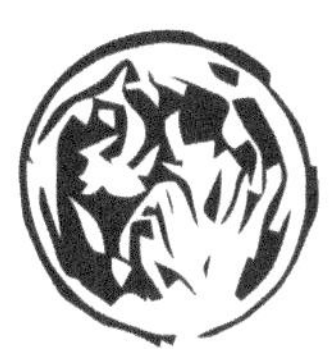

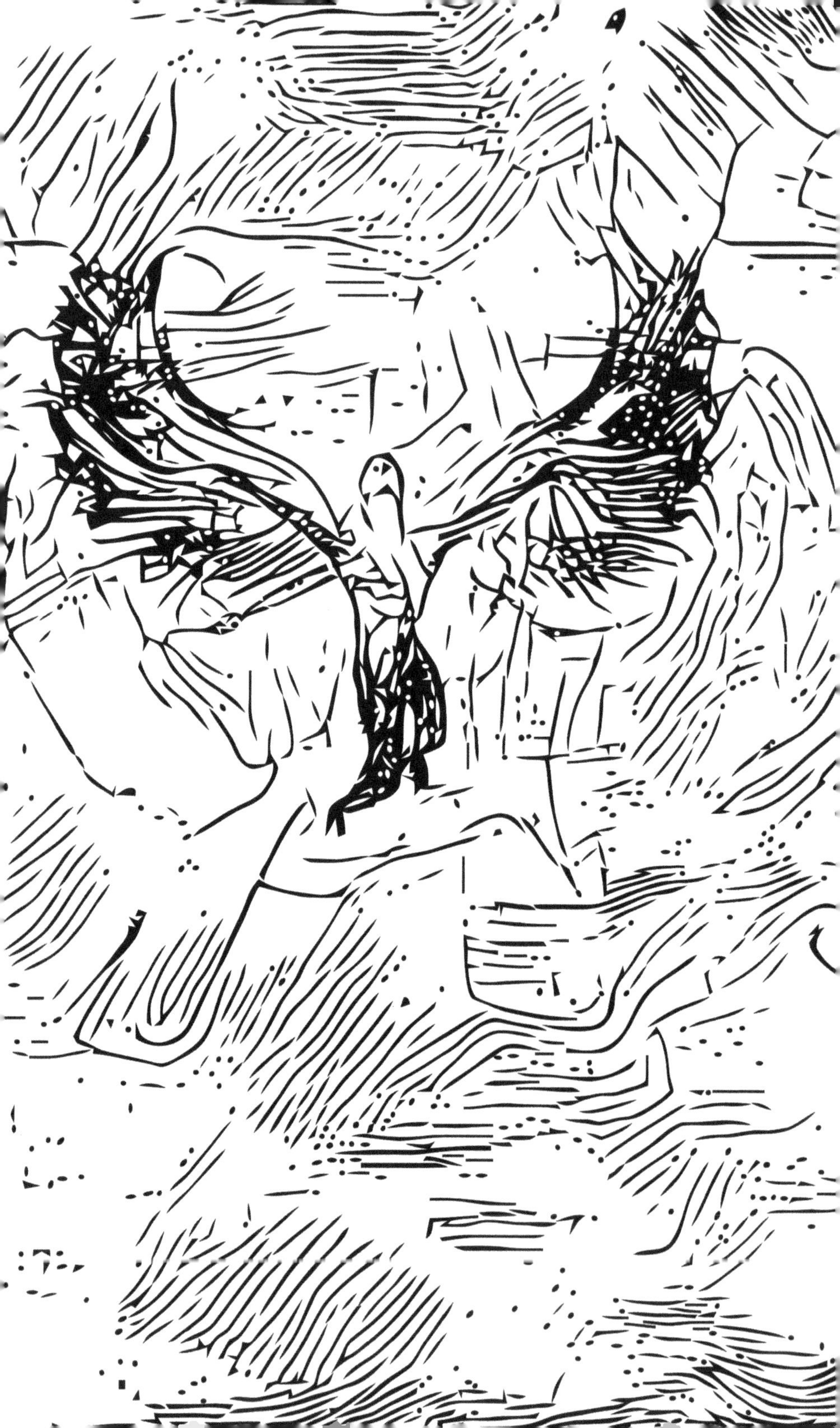

raven-winged Icarus
flies into the sun
defies myth
lives to cast his eye
into my heart

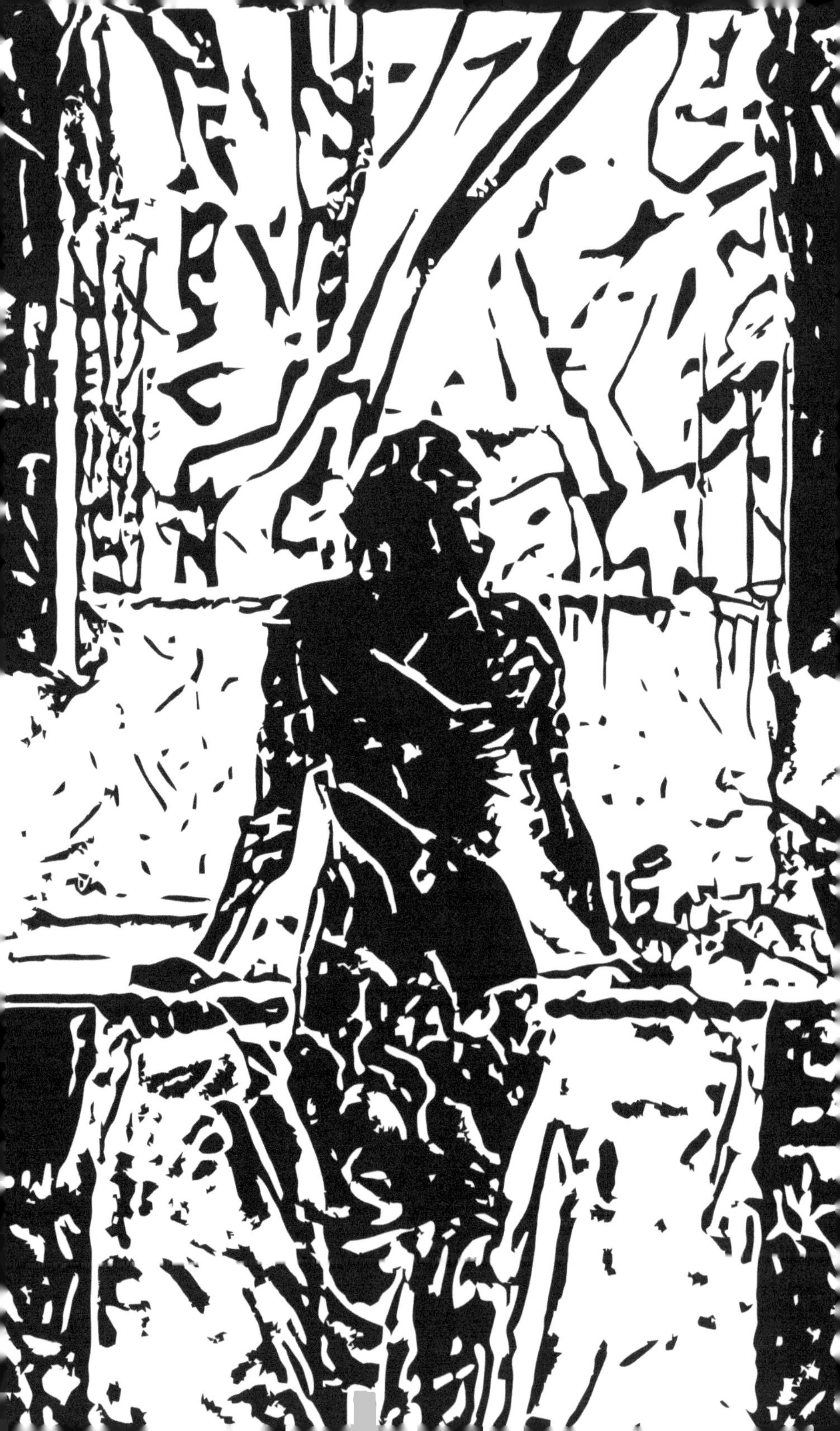

WINTER SOLSTICE:
PERSEPHONE'S RETURN

I stand at my kitchen window
in the silence of the still sleeping
house and watch the sun
scatter eucalyptus light into leaves,
peel red strips of sky from
smoothed trunks.
Naked in the morning.

Gathering up the shards of light,
I arrange them into day, work,
and they emerge
into sudden brilliance.
Jays flash blue glints.
The sun warms my back.

The winter garden grows green,
all leaves. A single turnip
purples the earth where I dig
into clumped earth, press clay,
mold the vessel that gathers the rain.
The birds drink from the earthen moon.

Evening, I hold the water-colored
sky bowl in my hands, descend
as daughter of the earth, and dream,
as the moon rises, tipping
the bowl, awakening to each return
of the day with crimson lips,

pomegranate seeds
still on my tongue.
When it grows light,
I will plant them.

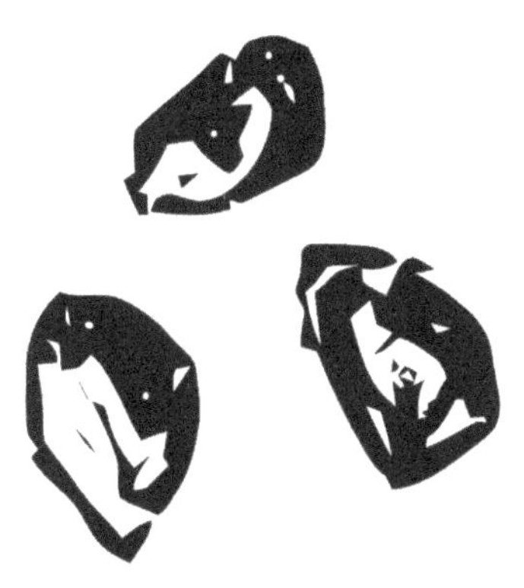

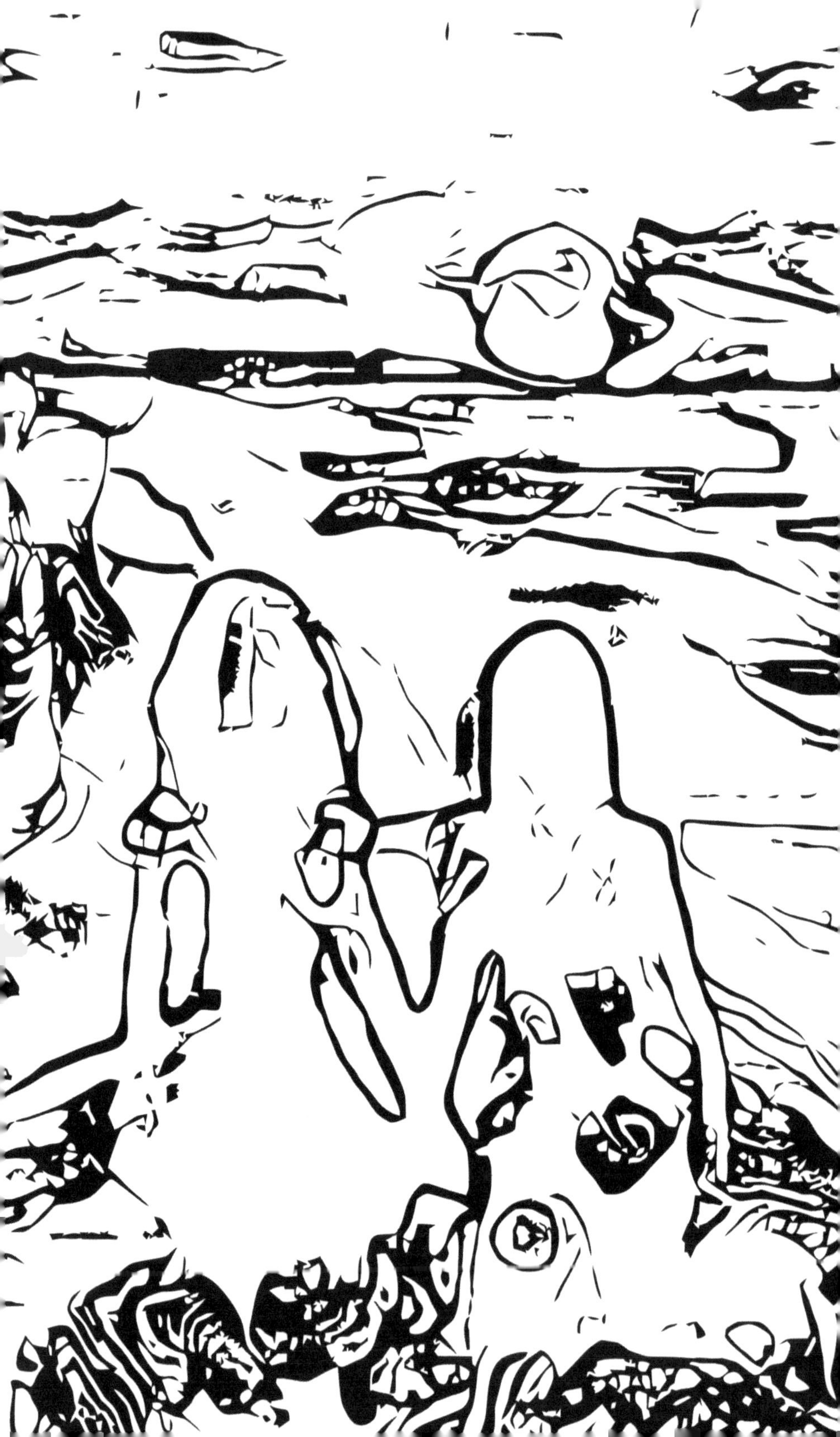

THEY DREAMED IN ENGLISH

a barely formed question
materializes in the crossed out words
who are you maia cruz palileo
I see you through the fronds of the night
guiding us, as we walk for hours, the two of us
hand in hand looking for the answer
wild flowers are blooming
and as we look again
the crossed out words repeat themselves
emerging in two languages
we walk together and the words speak
under the tender spell of dusk
no stars yet showing as we walk
but we now know the answer
as we have known all along is
the waves of the sea

(Based on the titles of paintings by Maia Cruz Palileo)

"I, CLAUDE MONET"

Look through reality
look until reality blurs the
colors of the sun
look until the colors rise
burning with morning
then blaze in the heat of the day
keep looking until the heat dissipates
and you find in your palette the burnished
gold and bold bronzes of the almost sunset
then watch until the sun fades
leaving the castle at Rouen
and the rivers of Paris
and London
and the bridge in your garden
almost indistinguishable
from the sky
all muted into the
grayblues
    that finally
        disappear
            into night.

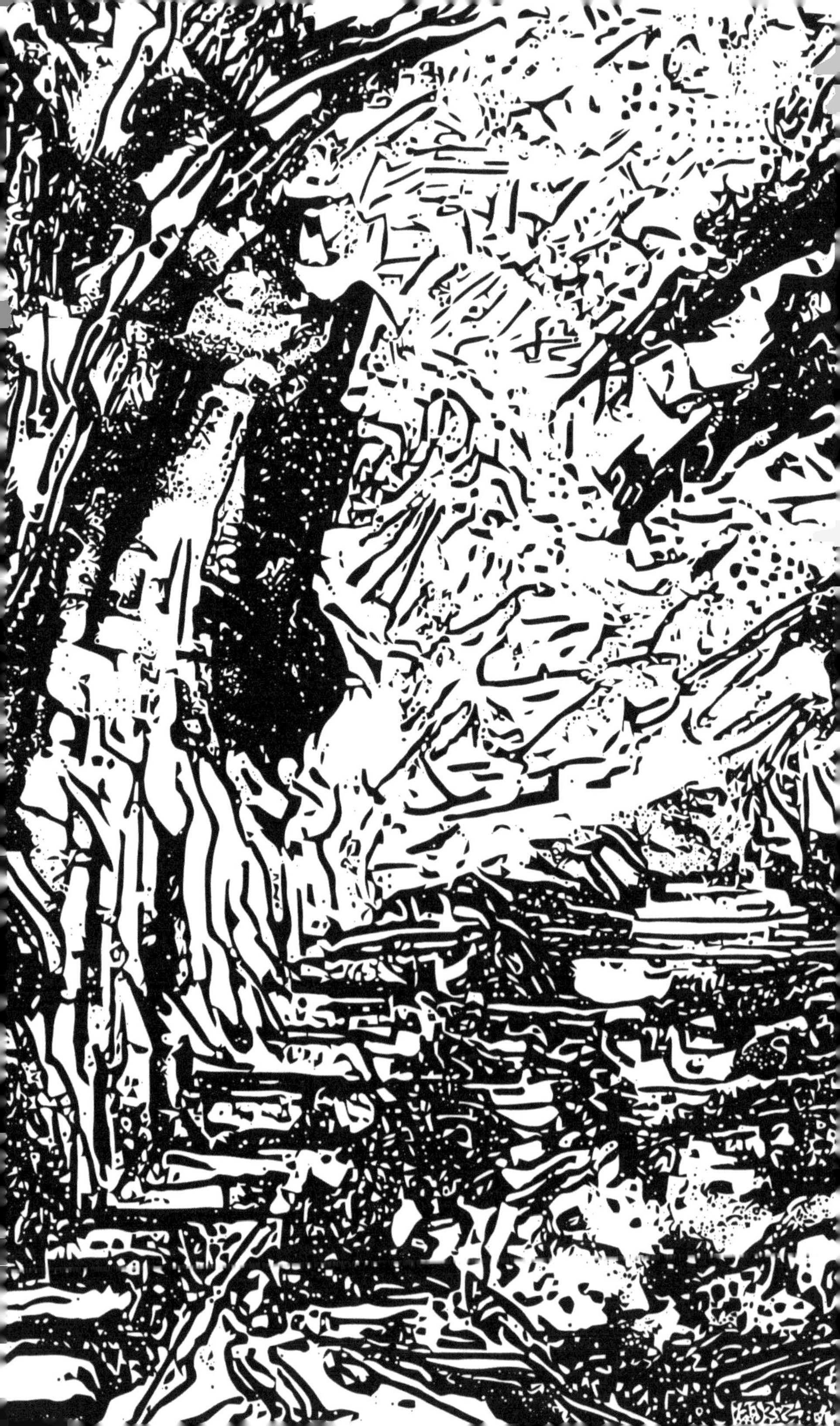

EKPHRASTIC RENDERING OF A PAINTING BY MATSUMI KANEMITSU

The artist's intent
appears in the last dream
ablaze in white space
naked as sun
nothing to contain the silence

Recognition illumines
scatters steps consumed by fire
spinning in dark ice reality
what is eternal does not speak
is known only before morning

before light erases the moon
before voice interrupts the dream
the shadowed sun returns to brilliance
as blossoms emerge
and sound becomes birdsong

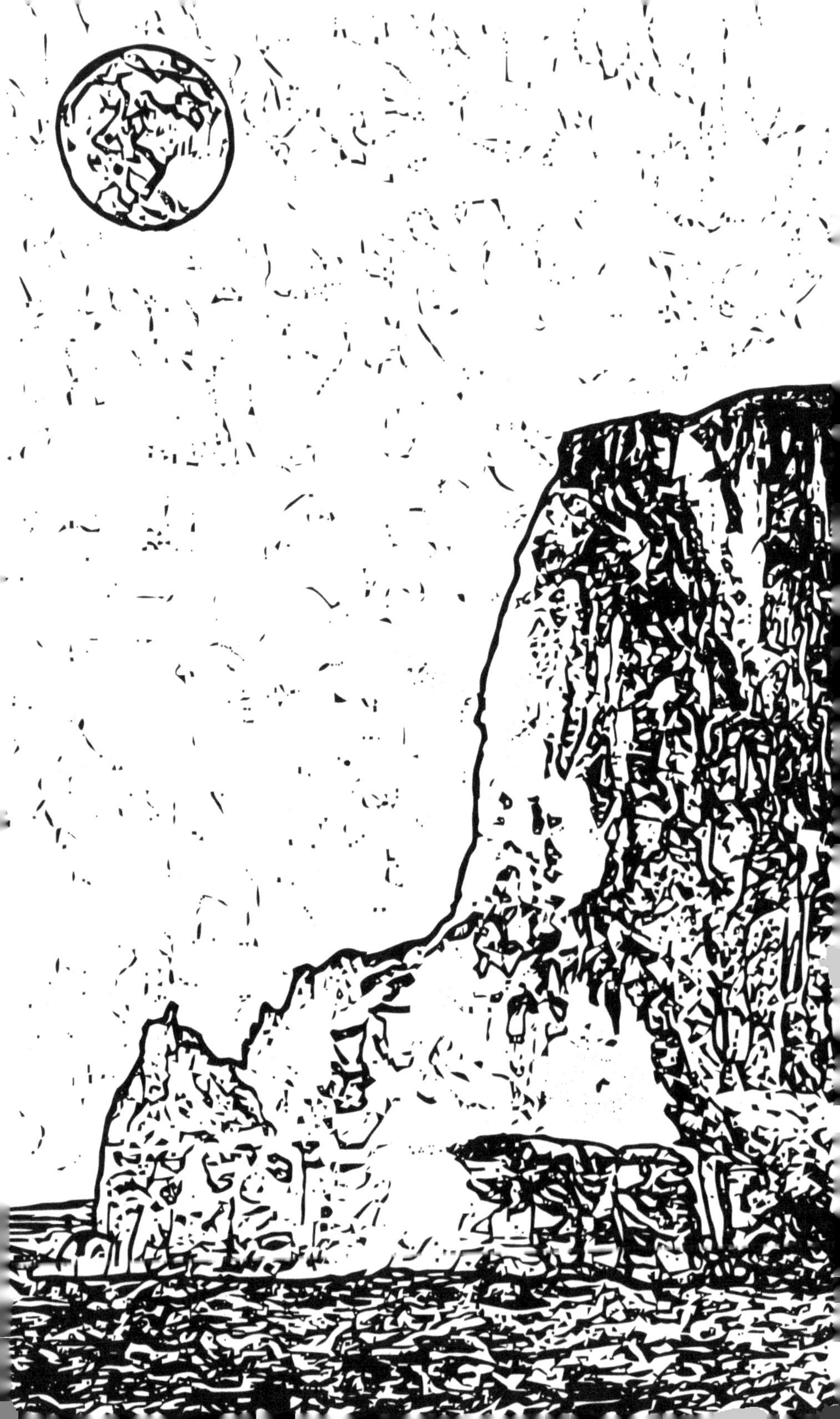

BRUSH STROKES

The Chinese artist knew
The brush to use, what tip
For the bamboo, what angle
For the wrinkled rock.
Their word, not mine,
The 'wrinkled' there with
Massive stone, evoking life
From cliffs that weather
Tides, grow fine lines etched
To hollows in the delicate brush
Of yesterday's many wrinkled moons.

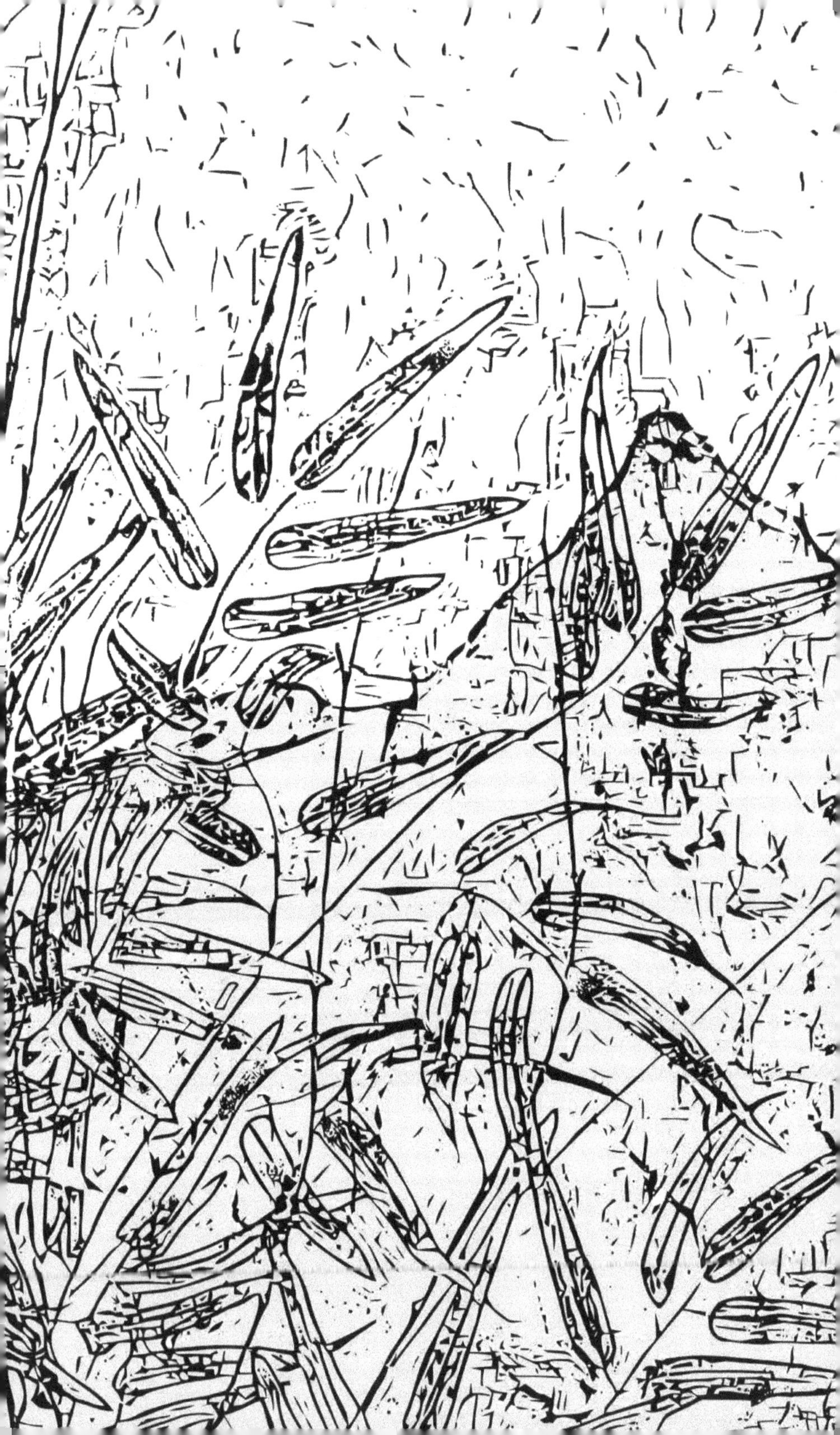

POEM HIDDEN IN BAMBOO

I dip my brush into the black Sumi ink,
point it against the side of the palette,
hold it, poised, above the delicate rice paper,
then add one leaf to the bamboo.
Then another. Over and over,
the leaves give shape to the branch,
the trunk, which arches left to right, bends
in the breeze we do not see.

The effects are there, on the paper,
the wind known only by what it touches.
The bamboo grows in earth we do not see,
do not paint. The space defines what lies beyond,
the path through the village, into the cleft
between the mountains.

None of this is visible.
Only the bamboo
and a stroke designating the edge
of the snow cap on the mountain
we know is there.

A SENSE OF PERMANENCE

the first house
three dawn redwoods
a bulwark
in front of the house
a magical protection

they stood as redwoods do
straight and tall
drawn to a silent drumming
we looked closely
found acorns secreted

woodpeckers
burrowing their future
where it lies
untouched by wind
rain or season

now this last house
three ancient redwoods
reenact their
heritage of long ago
bear witness

to the lives that have come
and the lives
that will go
untouched by moon
or season

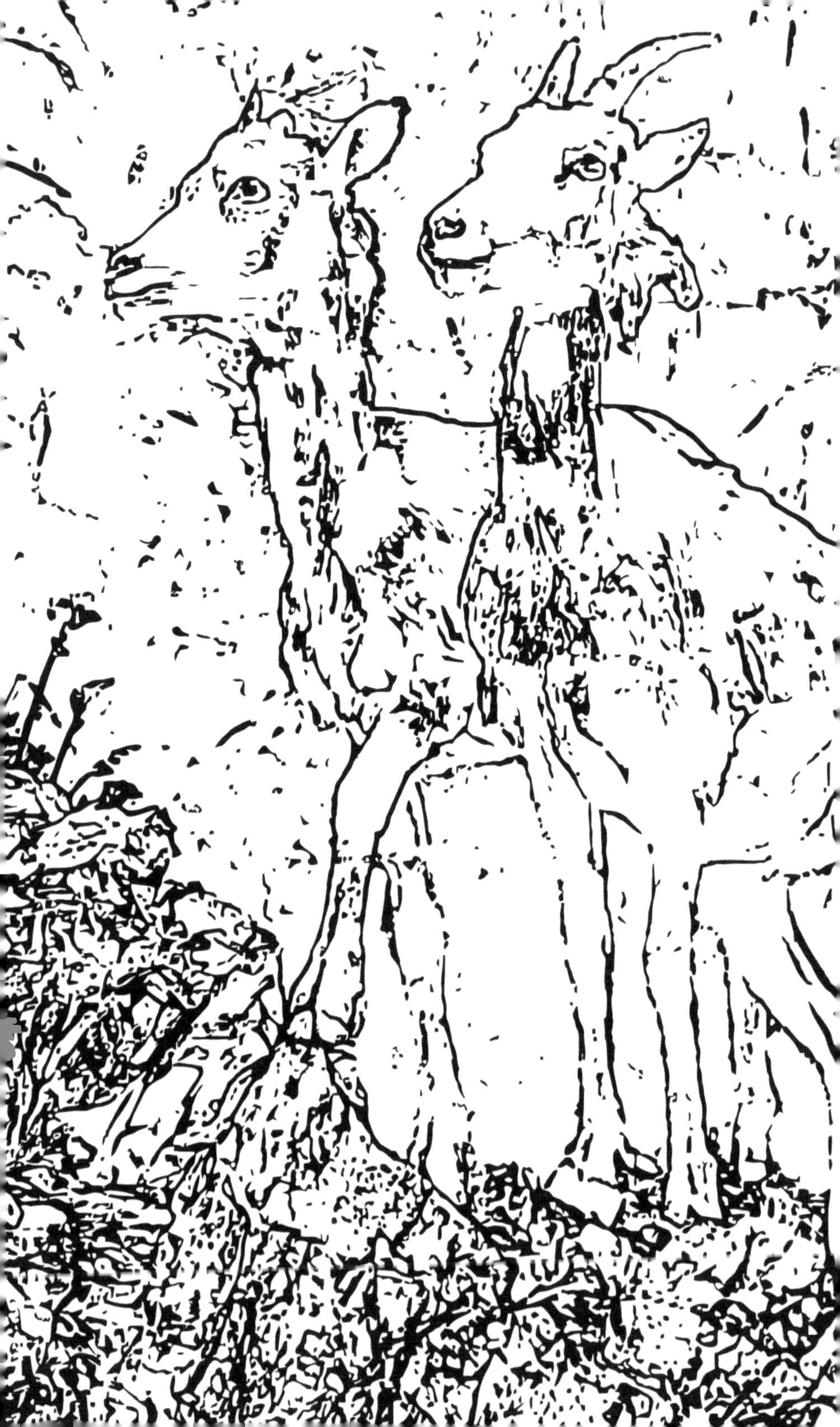

WHAT IS IT ABOUT THESE SHEEP?

What is it about these
shaggy mountain sheep
that holds my heart
in abeyance

sheep I have never seen
but a photographer I know
a man whose vision
expands my own

he saw in these sheep
the power of the lifted hoof

how is it that he can give to me
the eye of knowledge
sacred to these sheep
who live their lives

poised on the edge
            of awareness

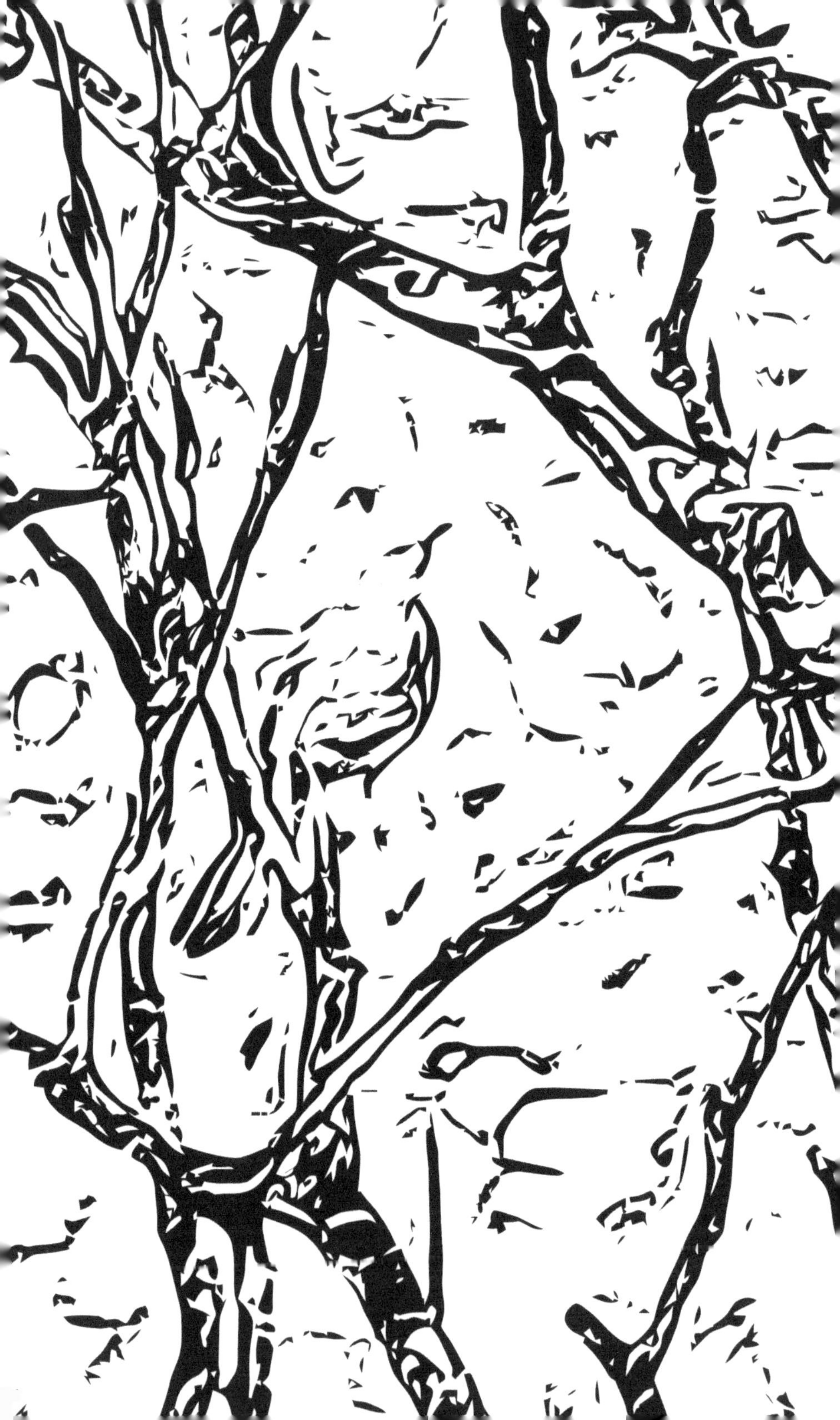

now that leaves
obscure the branches
you, too, are hidden
and I am left
with only your voice

mockingbird
sings in runes
no spaces
between the notes
your song

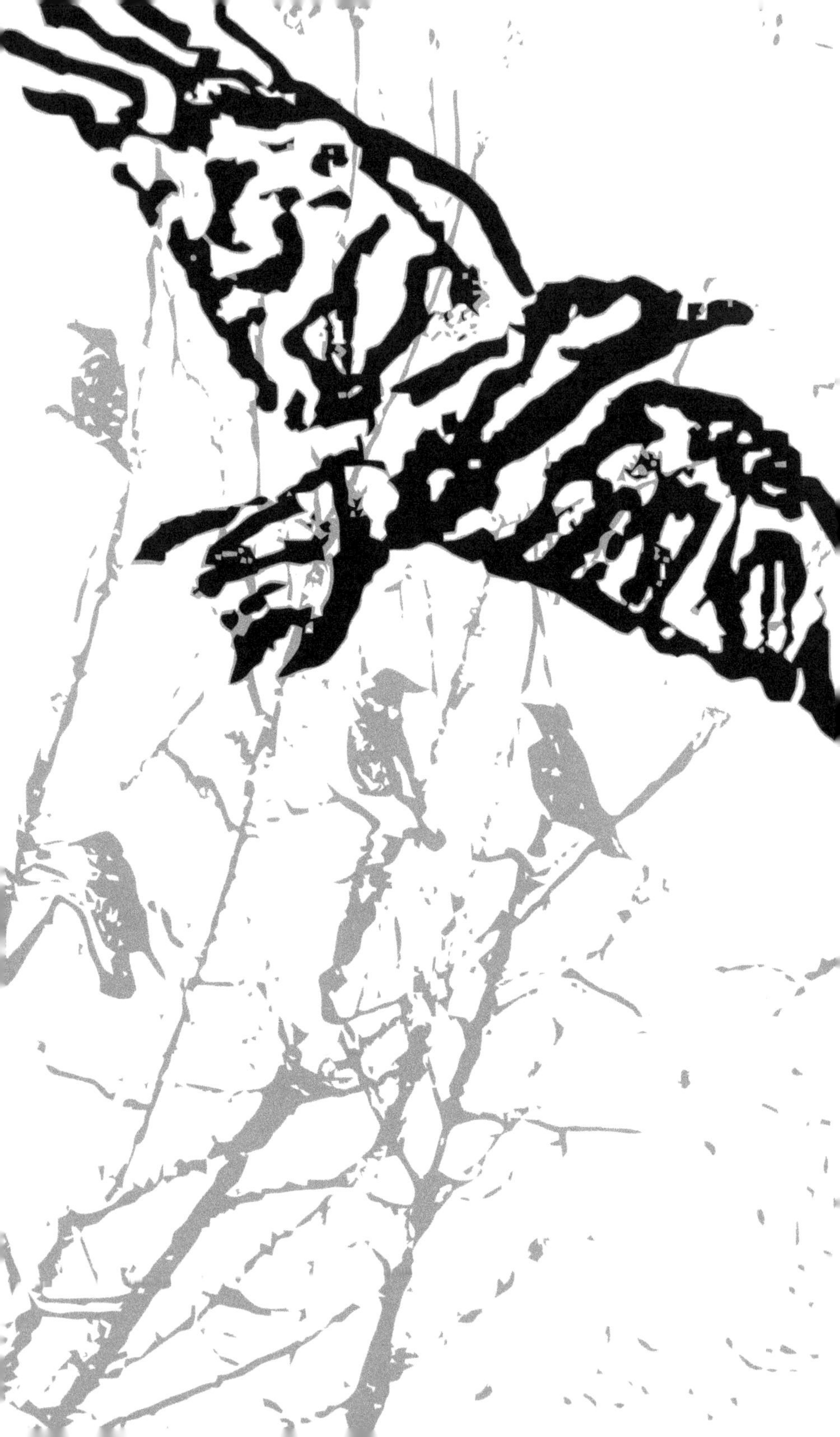

WINTER SOLSTICE IN SHADOW

I had just about given up hope
for color and song
but here they are
the birds that were ever-present
in our ancient apple trees

suddenly
in the dark heart of the year
color on black branches
in the bare willow
across the fence

I had not seen them here before
the cedar waxwings settling
as if they had just returned
while the crow flew high
embraced by sky

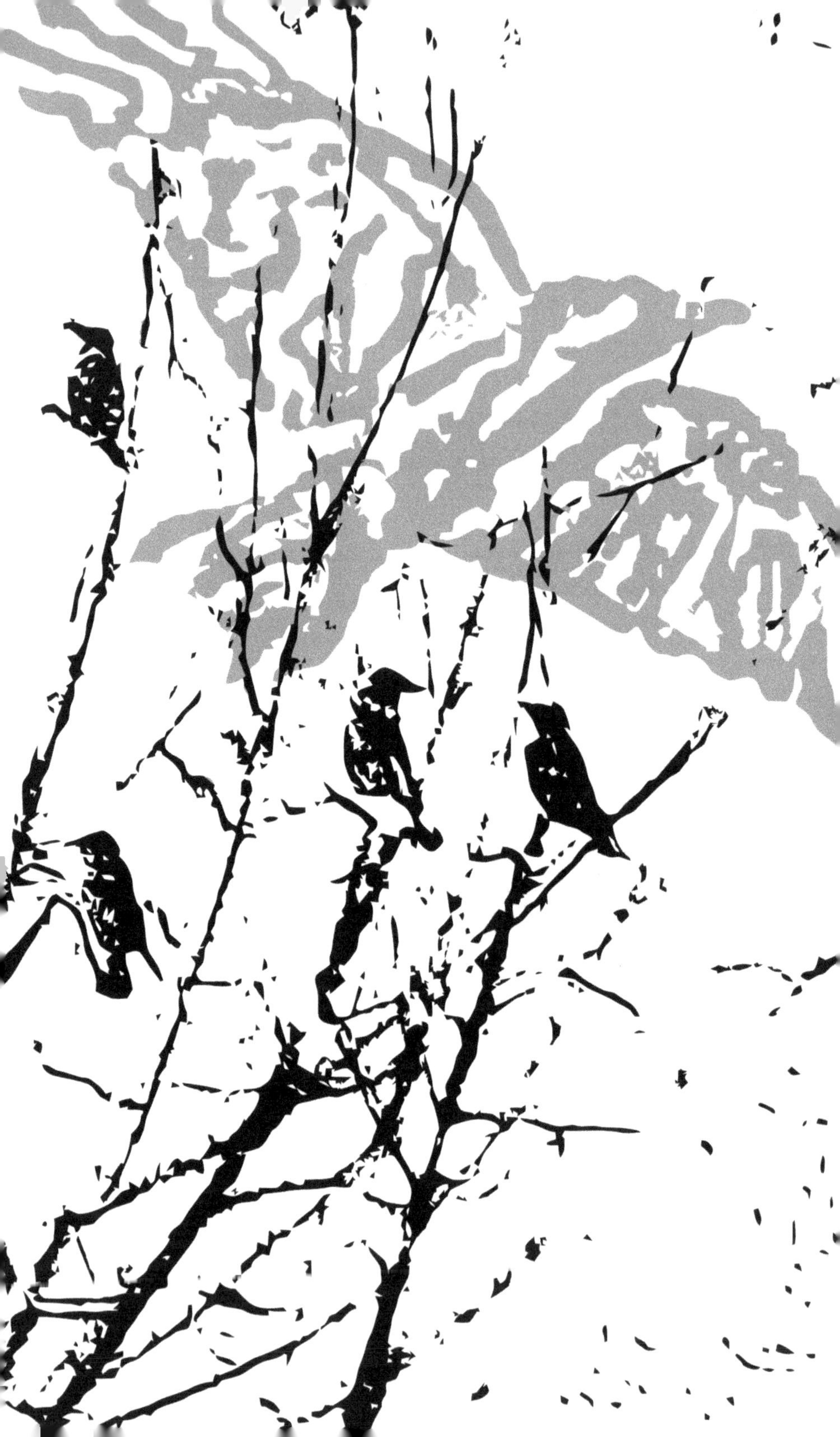

WINTER SOLSTICE

The dark heart of the year
brought birds to the bare willow
across the fence.

The crow, embraced by sky,
flew into the redwoods, leaving
black branches for the cedar waxwings
I had not seen here before.

I had just about given up hope, missing
the birds that were ever-present
in the orchard that housed our earlier home.
But here they are–filling this dark heart
of day with color and song.

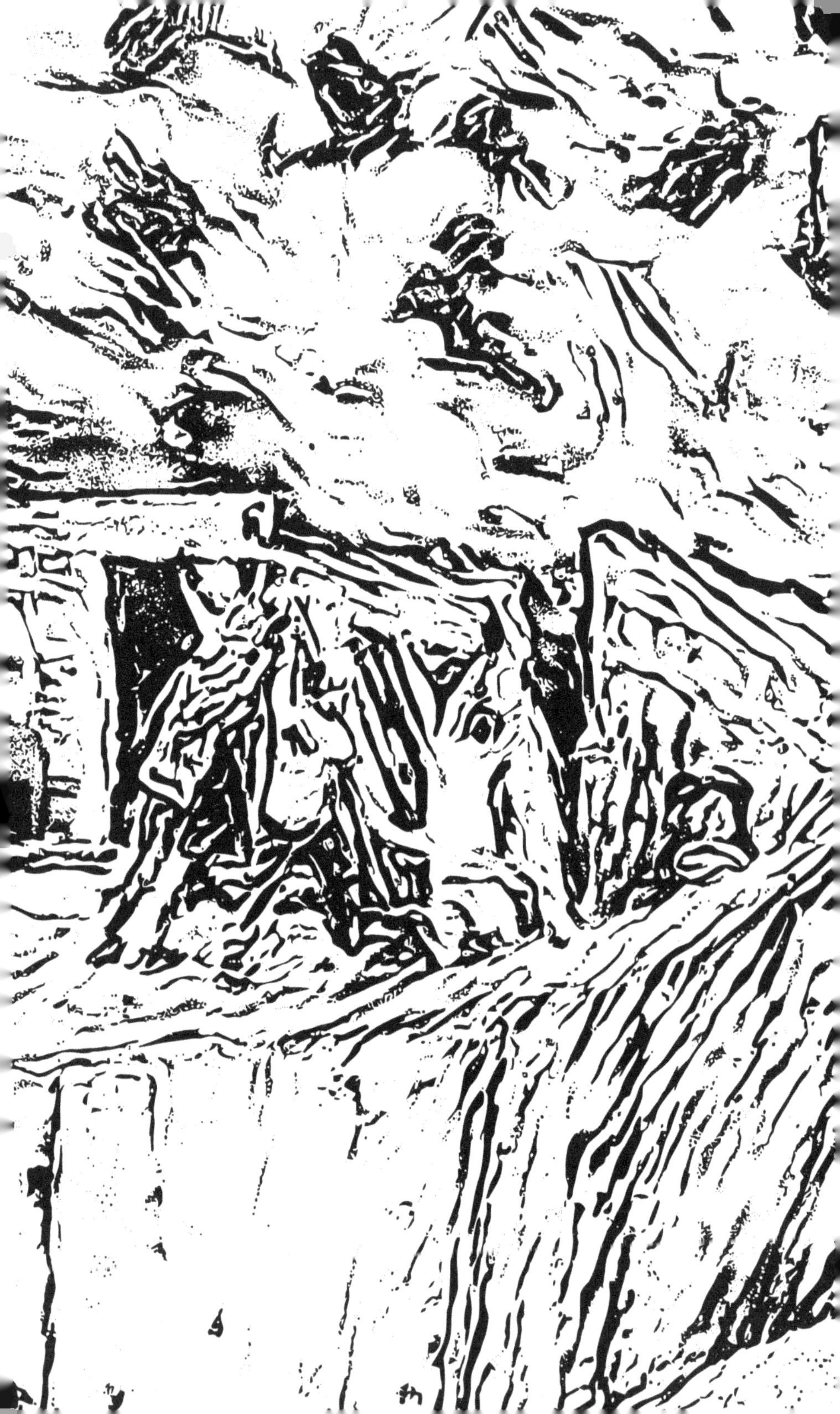

EVOLUTION OF THE SUN-TEMPLE

It began in the mind, the circle
that would both enclose and project the eye.
Reality, weeds. Knee high,
stickery weeds. In the mind
a smooth circle.

Even the approach is different.
The first glimpse, dropping
down the steep place in the road, shows
the moss-green irregular circle
enclosing space, bringing it into the house,
extending it beyond.

Reality, a water-tank across the road.
In the mind, a fence, just high enough
to obscure the tank, preserve the bank
of eucalyptus trees.

Reality, joggers and drivers, peering
in through glass walls, strangers' eyes
lighting on the blue Chinese prayer rug,
the hanging basket from Mexico,
the stained-glass window
catching and changing the sun.
In the mind, the moss-green fence,
joggers and cars reduced to eyeless sound.

The base, a circle of stone and cement
radiating out in arcs. Round piling posts,
washed green, sunk into earth. Then the
rough lumber sawed, curved, each board

cut to fit in one place only. Panels rising,
grooved, stained.

The Circle, you called it
until the neighbor, a Nobel physicist,
walked his dog into the half-finished space.
Sun-temple, he muttered, aging giant of a mind,
poking around, examining, eye to microscope,
stumping off, satisfied.

That, too, you said,
as you finished the inner circle, emptying the
burlap bags of stones we had gathered from the beach
one by one, washed up by the tides for just this place
all these years later.

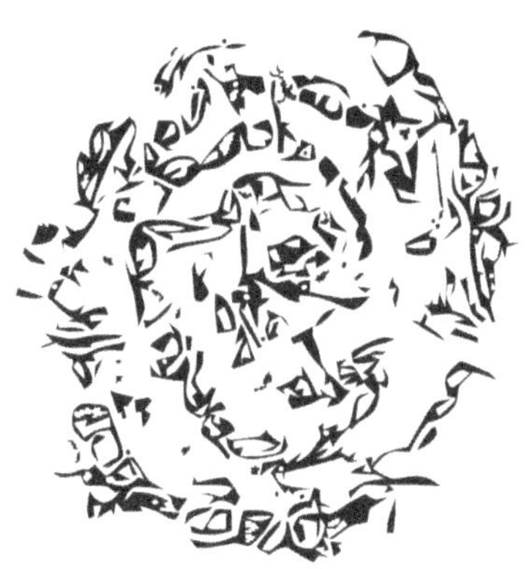

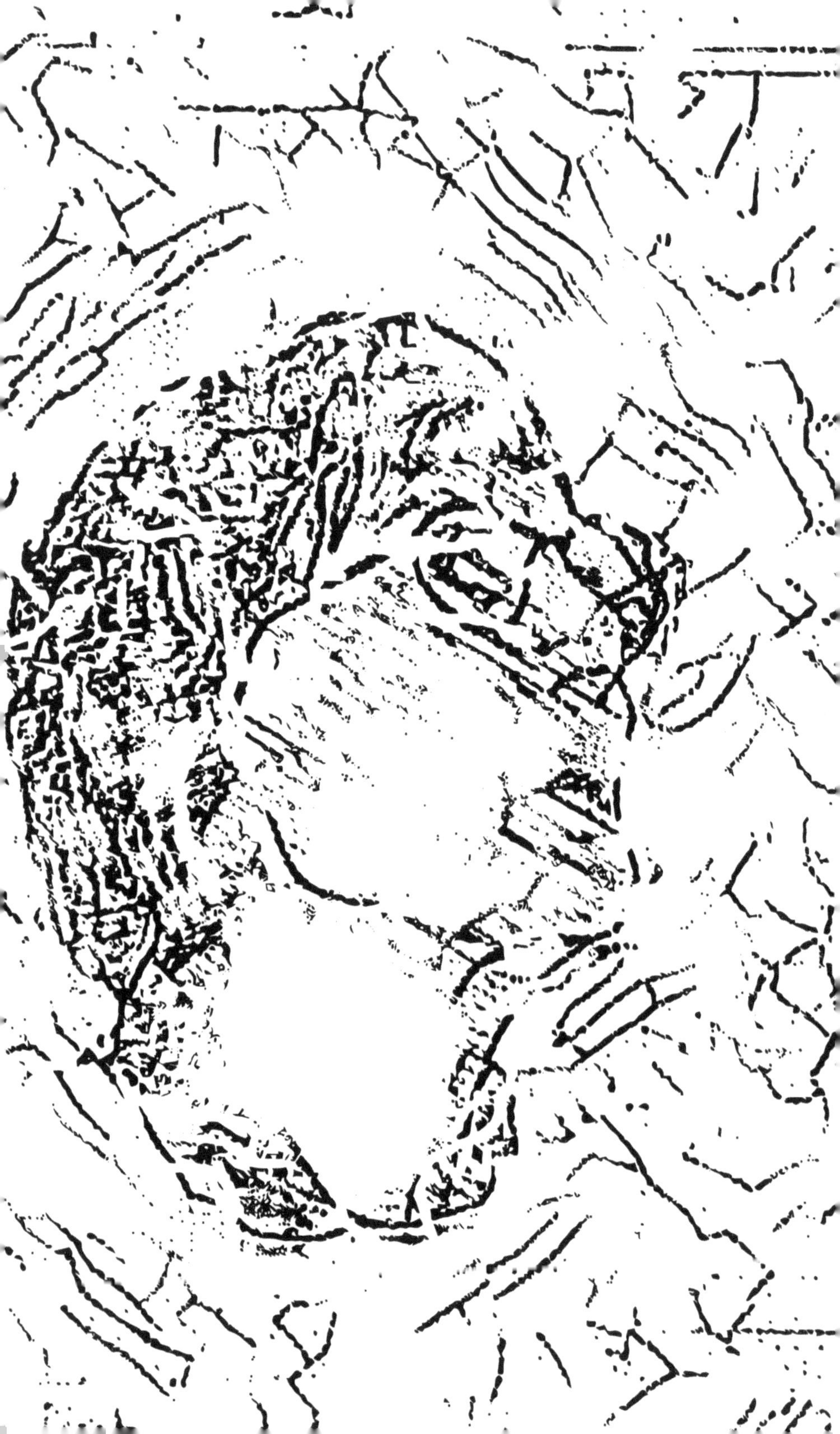

AUBADE FOR THE QUIET HOUSE

I awaken to a still-dark room
No sound to acknowledge a new day
No sense of the dream that woke me

The silent saluki across my feet
is, like me, not moving but awake
His eyes as always awaiting my move

Was it like this yesterday
and the day before
dreamless dark and silent

Will it be like this tomorrow
or will we be able to move freely
call out an aubade to the morning

Open to what once was as natural
as the sun falling across your face
as natural as another day of living

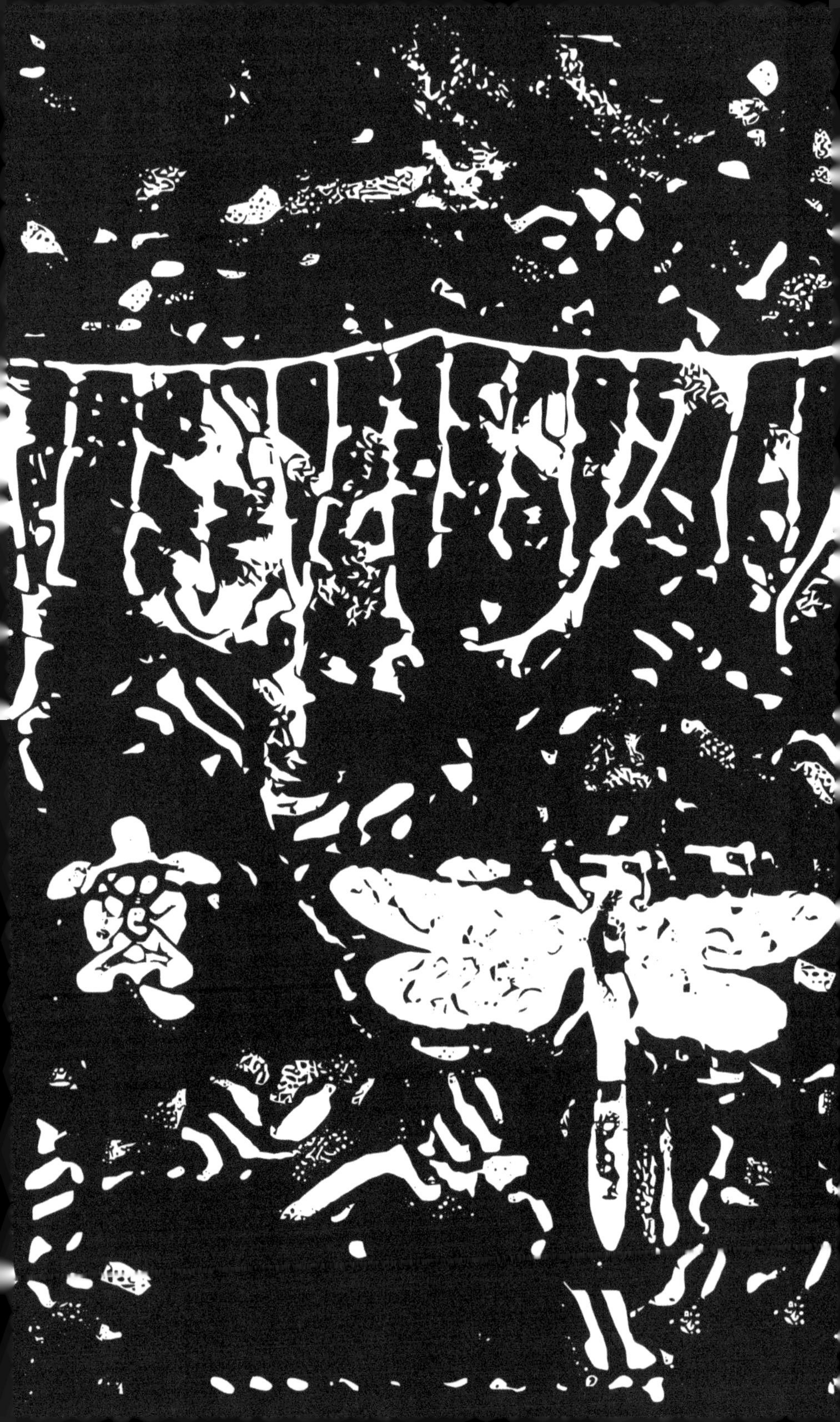

FLICKERING LIGHTS

I would write a poem for you
a poem without time or distance
a poem hidden in a potted orchid
above a yellow and lavender tablecloth
about to blossom

the rose clings to the petaled earth
dark chocolate supports
a flotilla of marshmallows
distortions of reality
animate moons

in this small yard
no walnut husks or persimmons
hang on black boughs
no trace of ice on this deck
to note the prints of afghan hounds
marking the day that snow
obscured November

I would write a poem for you
a poem without time or distance
but look
the lights you hung
on the fence
still flicker silently
until the sun turns them off

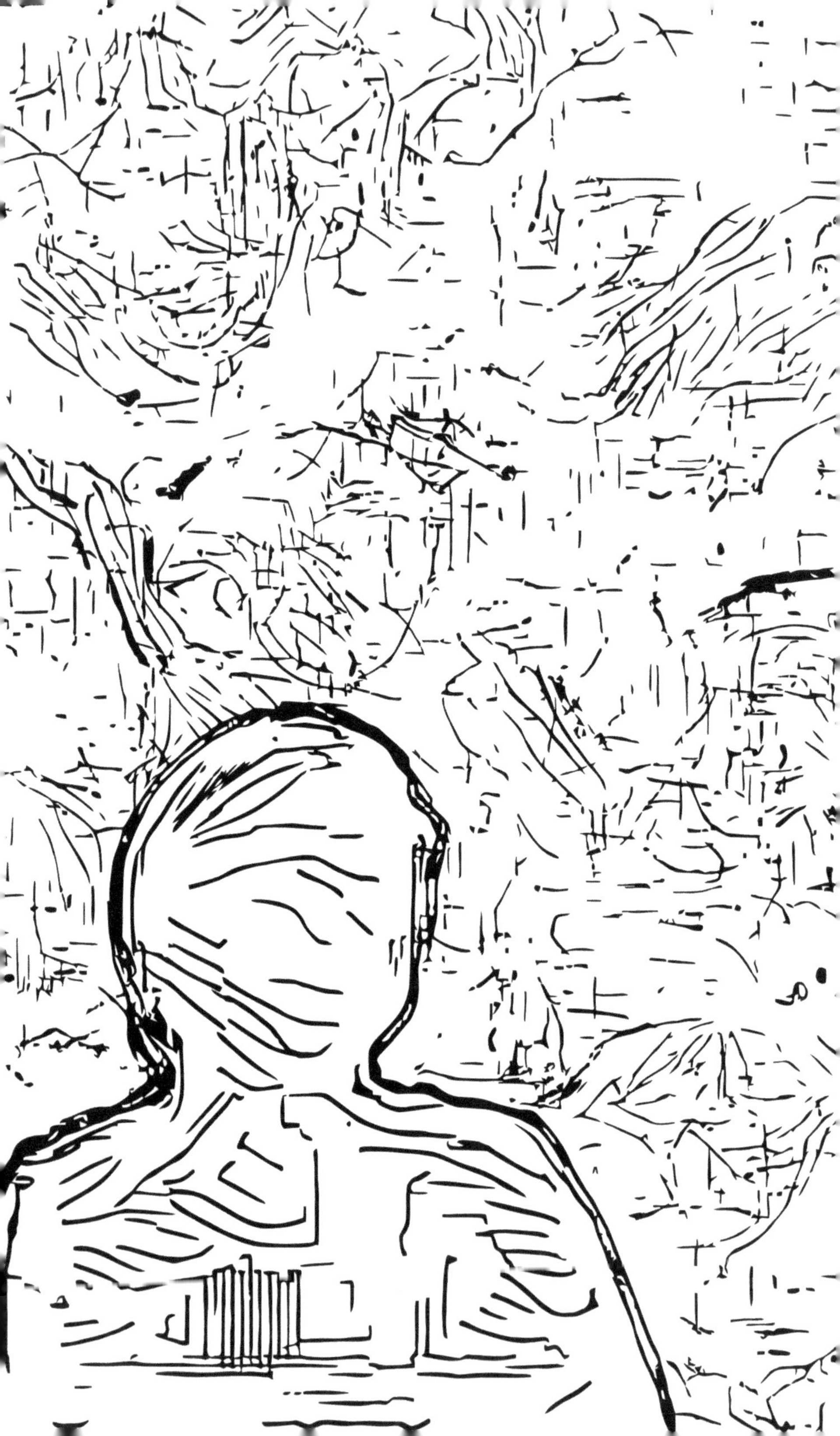

A FIELD GUIDE TO MEMORY

I The Birdwoman

No one else is alive
who remembers.
The future in the poem
is not beholden to its past.

Carefully I fill in the dates in April
only one birthday there
but March was busy with birthdays
and doctors

It is March and the poinsettia's red leaves
are still hanging, creating a future
that may outlast
the calendar.

Departures from the ordinary
the familiar, the prosaic, art
as technique, predictable as neurons
in the hippocampus

Move in the direction of tropes
undefined miracles, secrets, myths
Notice the visible quality of silence
drawing the line over the unsaid.

End with the image, don't explain.
The birdwoman
stands by the window
dreaming in cloud cover.

II Saying the Unsaid

Birdwoman returns
        stands at the window
        waiting
No, she hears, go to the door,
        open it.
Far in the distance
        flash of movement
then
        stillness
                silence.
She turns
        sees in the window
what lives in the silence
        what was always there
beside her--
                his relentless devotion

for Madgik, August 1, 2009 - August 5, 2022

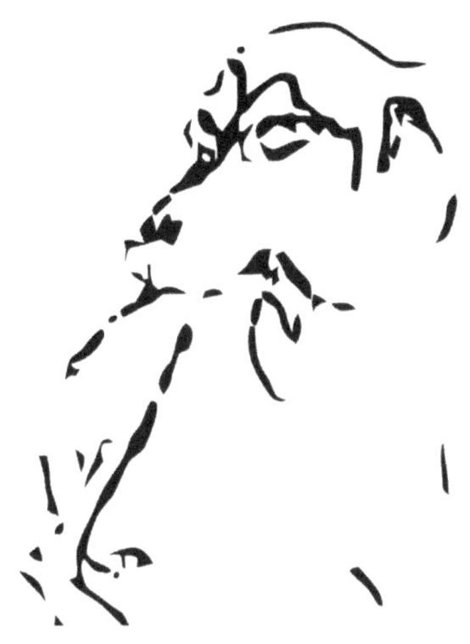

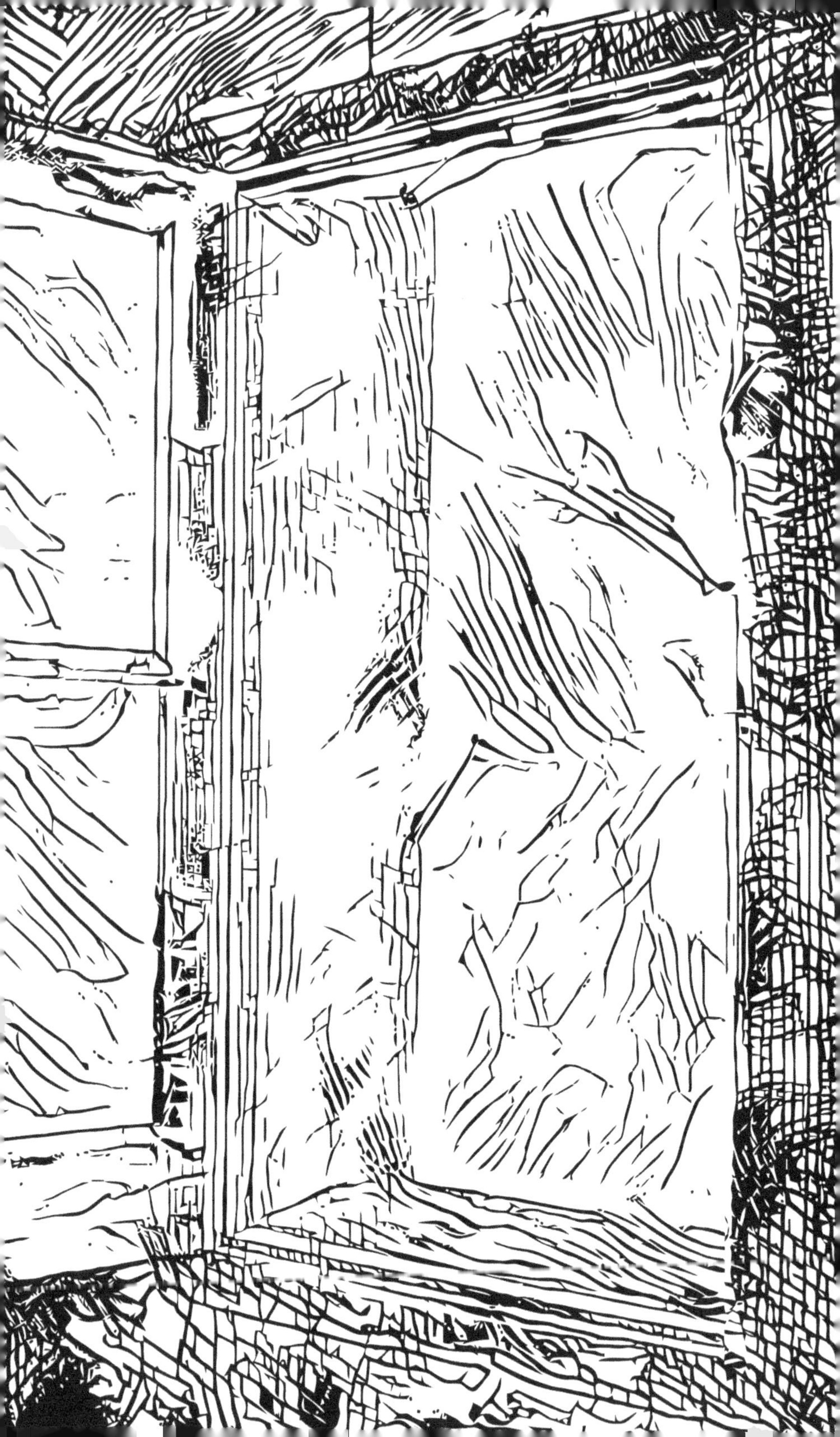

Oh, empty ledge
where once you landed
so briefly
my heart remembers
the beat of your wings

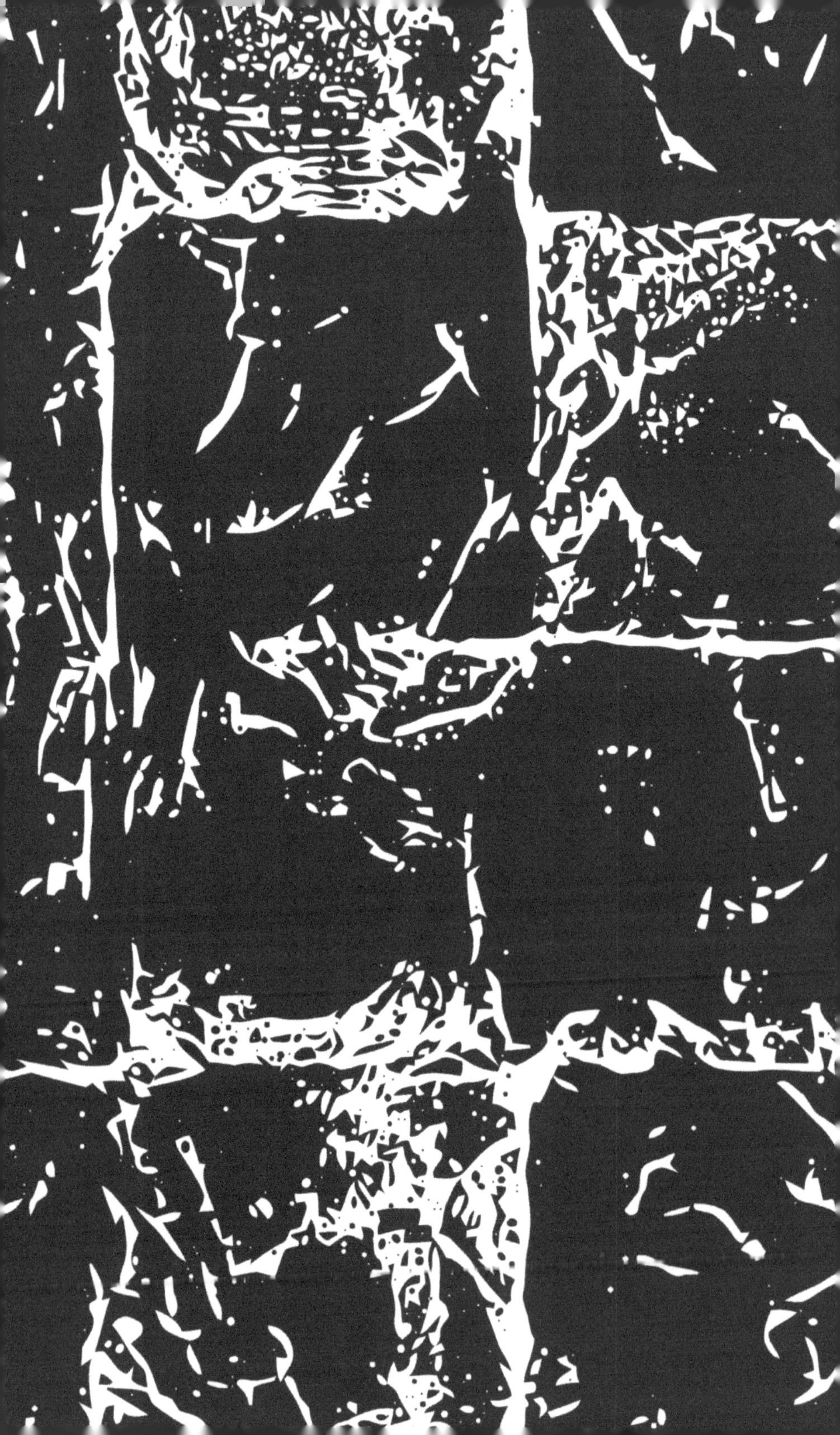

LITANY

For all that is done and said
We know their dream; enough
to know they are dreamed and are dead

from Yeats' "Easter, 1916"

Enough to know.
They are dreamed
And are dead
The litany in my head
utters their names
one by one.
Dead. Not dead.
Dreamed.
The beginning. Kneel down
on the cold stone floor
of my dreams.
The stone of the heart recalls first
the great-grandmother's name:
Flora, from the isle of Tiree,
who brought with her to Ohio,
knowledge of Latin and Greek,
and the words of Shakespeare
Far from the Scottish Hebrides
Flora's son Donald, and Mary,
his young bride from Wales,
started their family
and Mary gave birth
to Marietta Walker,
first of their twelve children
Then Donald, their son named
after his father.

Then Carrie. Bill. Sam. Norval.
The family grew, boys
following their father
Into the coal-dark days.
The girls stayed in school
like their grandmother from Tiree.
They lost a child, Kenneth,
dead from typhoid.
Then came Maggie May,
the middle child,
(Maggie May, Margaret, Midge-
All names worn by my mother.)
followed by Mary Elizabeth (Betty).
Elbert. Lucy Florence.
And the youngest, Robert.
Twelve children
and never an angry word
in that household.
The names go on,
but my knees,
on that ancient stone
known only to memory,
have no feeling.
Only telling.
The names
come faster.
They are harder to say.
The brothers.
Dale, Don, Bill.
The cousins.
Their children
and their children
And now, in silence,

the stone.
My heart.
My love.
Say it.
Enough to know.
Dreamed.
And dead

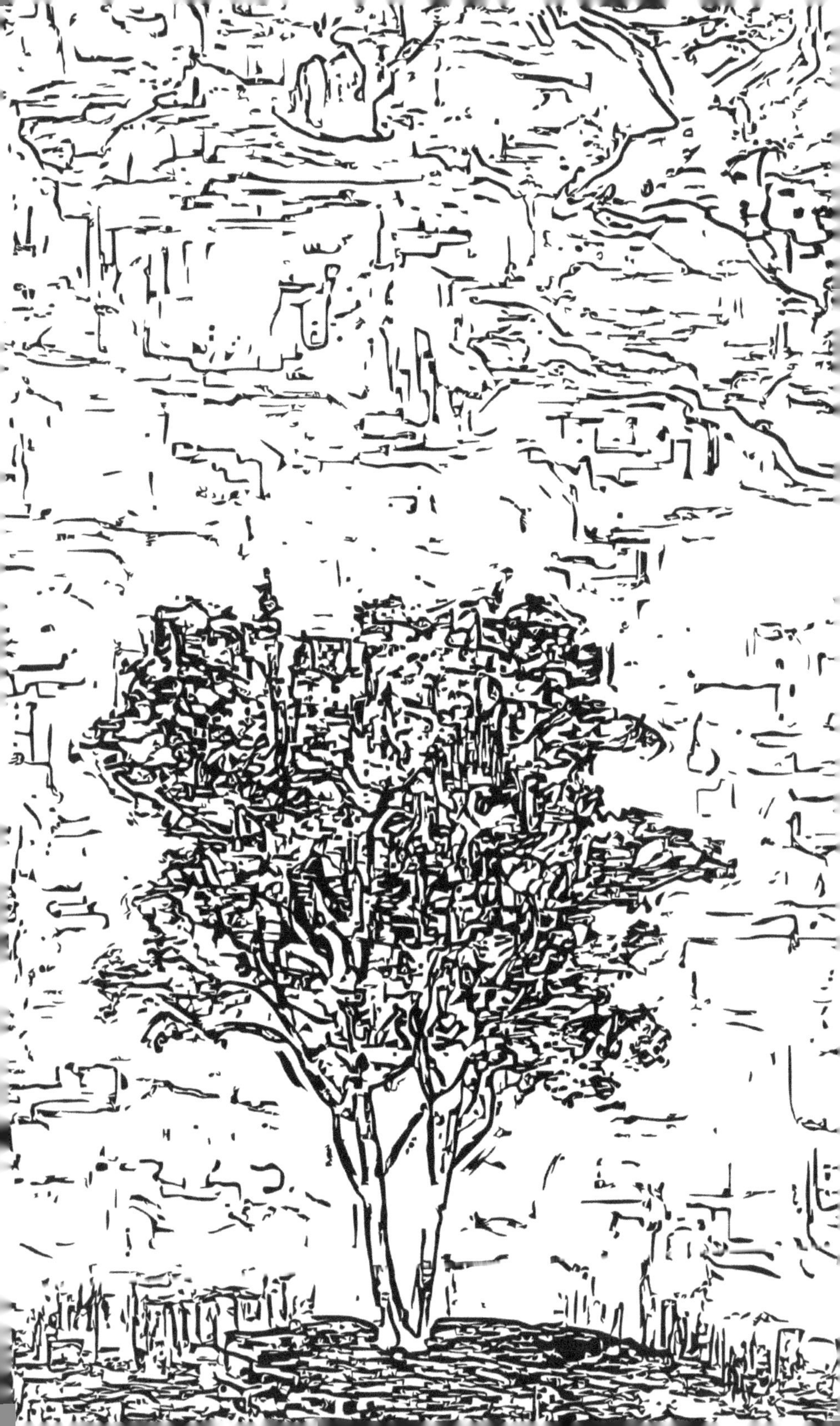

IN TIMES LIKE THESE

In Times like These,
It is Necessary to Talk about Trees.

Adrienne Rich

I

In Times Like These

Listen.
You are overwhelmed.
You are unprepared.
You are terrified.
But open the window.
Listen to the voices outside.
They have gathered there.
Your mothers your daughters
Your nieces. Your sons.
Yes, your sons and most
clear most articulate
most anguished---
your sisters.

Put out your hand,
Let yourself be led
Away from the window
toward the door.

Listen, outside
you will hear the trees
you will hear the wind in the aspen

you will notice the silver undersides
of the poplar leaves.
Listen to the sounds of these trees.
Listen to Daphne tell of what she learned
as a laurel tree.

II

Daphne speaks

I once lived among the waters —
the rivers, the springs
a tidepool at the bottom of a waterfall.
My father Peneus, the river god
protected me from lustful Apollo

now my leaves bend to the wind
and I listen to the aspen, the poplar
these trees too have known
the waters of life

in this time of
cosmic upheaval
remember when you
were born of water and
ran with the naiads
along rivers and oceans

when you emerged
from mother earth you
like me were overwhelmed

terrified unprepared
for life without the
cool waters.

Life as a tree
gives stability and
communion
between earth and sky
My leaves change
and fall as I navigate
my world

listen
In these times
imagine possibility
walk the sands that surround you
notice the small

the sea anemone
affixed to rock in its watery home
see how it spreads its tendrils
of pale lapis and deep magenta
shades between those of the artist's palette

step into the tidepool
reclaim the waters of your birth

look to the frog
how it moves
the gathering in
the leap

the landing—
limbs folded
silent as stone

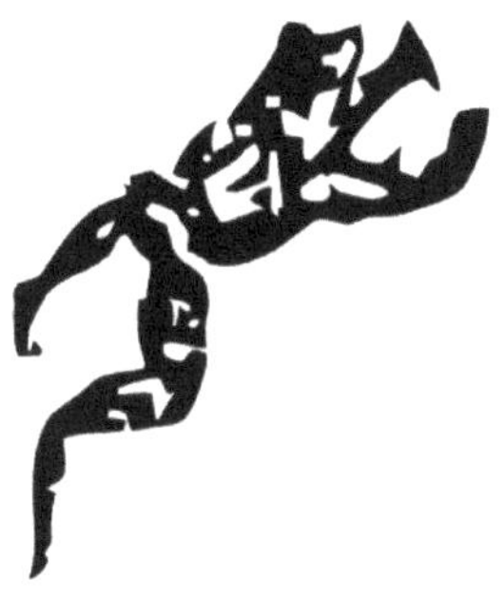

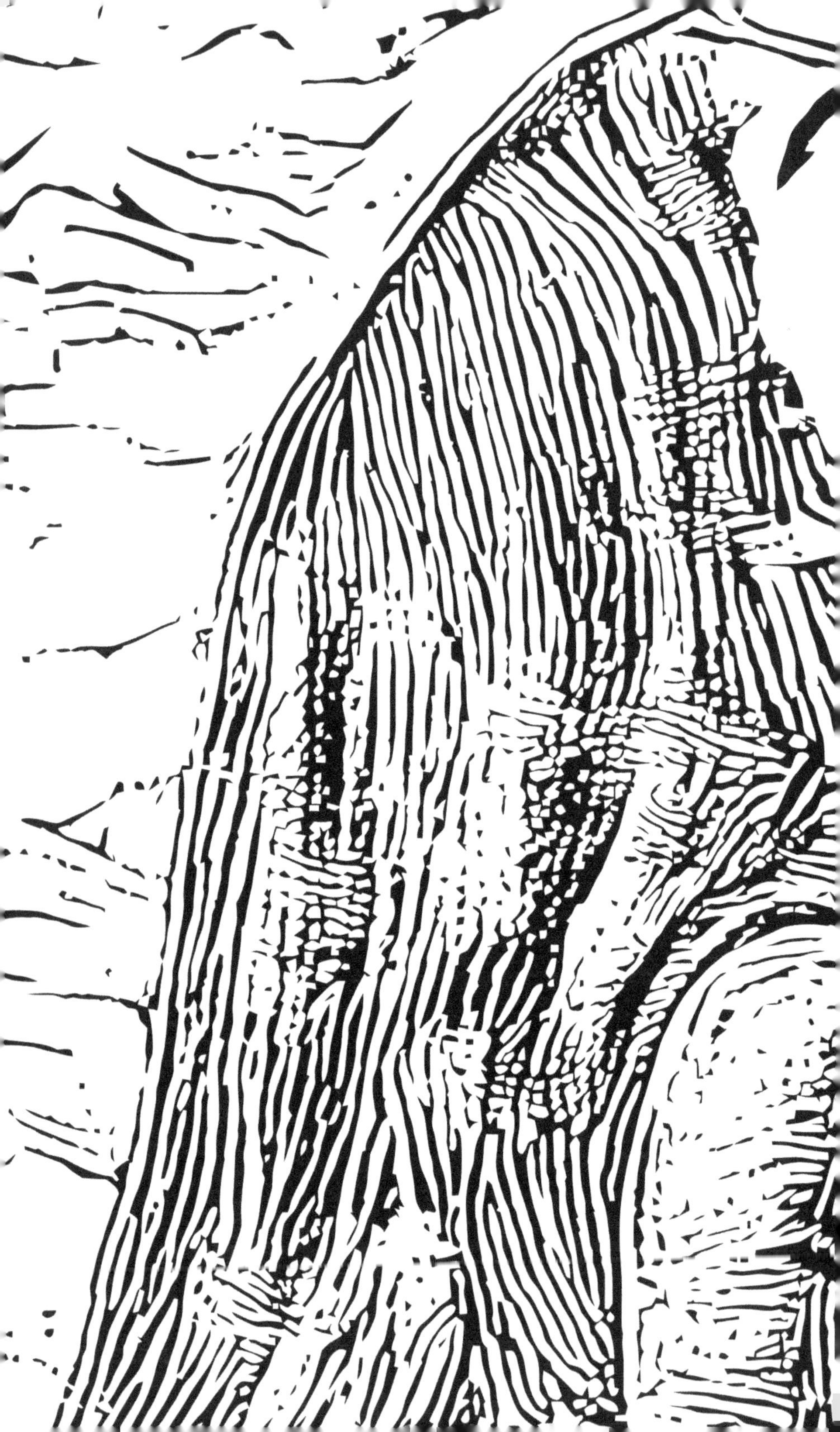

HOW TO PREVENT THE PULL OF GRAVITY

Spread silk over wool, birdwoman says.
Yes. Silk over wool.

Gravity pulls you to the earth, grounds you in this life.
Music. Friends. Wool.
(Spin, weave, give scarves to love.)

Hear heartbeat in wool. Know pulse. Rhythm of love.

Spread silk over wool.
Filter of light extracts essence.

Rainbow silk, prism of rough wool
holds (molds) the warp and the woof.
films the texture with the silk-screen of light.

Silk, spun out of air.
Life-stuff, moon-made, the birdwoman
spins words out of light:
(Rapunzel, Rapunzel, spin me a dream.
How do I know your name, princess of the long
golden hair, spun out of myth—
Arachne, Rapunzel, Chandra,)

Hold. Center on silk, spread over wool.
Gravity, Levity,
Right, left.
Center. Balance. Choose your space.
Fill it with light.
The light holds. The word, light, touches the heart of love.
(with love)
Spread silk. Over wool.

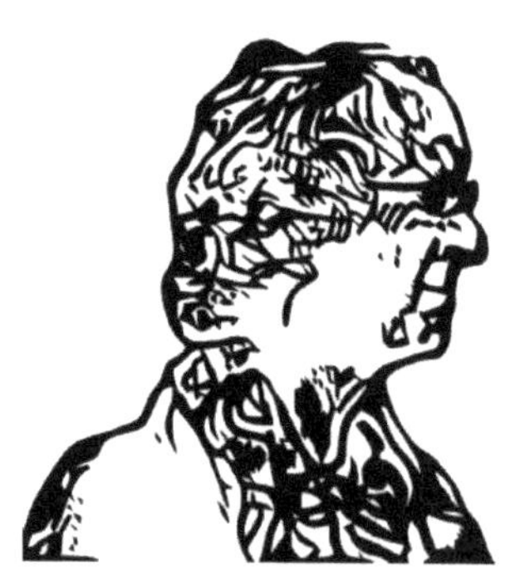

www.ingramcontent.com/pod-product-compliance
Lightning Source LLC
LaVergne TN
LVHW052355100826
845147LV00013B/852
9780990619772